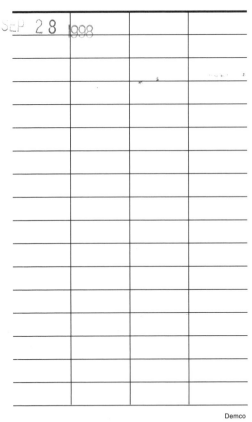

DATE DUE

SEP 28 1998			

Demco

Essay Index

Spirit of Delight

Spirit of Delight

By
George McLean Harper

Rarely, rarely, comest thou,
Spirit of Delight!

Essay Index Reprint Series

BOOKS FOR LIBRARIES PRESS
FREEPORT, NEW YORK

Essay Index

STANDARD BOOK NUMBER:

8369-0016-2

LIBRARY OF CONGRESS CATALOG CARD NUMBER:

78-76902

MANUFACTURED
BY
HALLMARK LITHOGRAPHERS, INC.
IN THE U.S.A.

To

ROBERT H. MARSH

AN ENGLISH FRIEND AND THEREFORE
FAITHFUL FRIEND OF MINE AND
OF MY COUNTRY

PREFACE

In all beautiful art, in all scientific discovery, in all creative activity whatsoever, the spirit of delight is manifest.

" And thence flows all that charms or ear or sight,
All melodies the echoes of that voice,
All colors a suffusion from that light."

But this is one side of a paradox, for much imaginative literature, especially in recent times, is extremely sad,— sadder, I hope, than life itself is for most people. The poets and romancers cherish their poignant woe, and perhaps in this trait we may perceive the other aspect of the paradox and thus begin to understand it. Keats, who must have been one of the happiest of mortals, knew the secret, and of Melancholy he sings:

" She dwells with Beauty — Beauty that must die;
And Joy, whose hand is ever at his lips
Bidding adieu."

With this hint from him we can dispel the shimmering illusion that he and the rest of the glad fellowship of artists have drawn before their laughing eyes. When they make beautiful things, like the " Ode on Melancholy " or Coleridge's "Dejection," or Shelley's "Stanzas Written in Dejection near Naples," it is in vain that they try to persuade us they are really unhappy. Achievements such as theirs redress the balance of human suffering, for a time at least and for them. They know that for the world also they can turn sorrow into song:

> "Ay, in the very temple of Delight
> Veil'd Melancholy has her sovran shrine."

And reversing the terms, they see that without delight there can be no successful creation. Did not one of them long ago sing: "And God saw the light that it was good"? The joy of creation comes but rarely, yet upon its coming the artist must wait, for without it he can do nothing. We wish to share his days of strength, his heroic hours, his moments of exalted pleasure.

Even so I hope these essays of mine about men and women who have added much to the joy and sweetness of life will themselves give forth a certain radiance. They were written joyously from time to time as I felt moved with admiration. The little sketches of travel, I may truly if humbly say, were caused by visitations of the spirit of delight, and are memorials of wanderings with her whose happy touches in "Mycenæ" I proudly acknowledge as the best part of that narrative.

I thank the publishers of the Quarterly Review (London), the Atlantic Monthly, Scribner's Magazine, the Sewanee Review, and the Virginia Quarterly Review for permission to reprint some of the articles.

G. M. H.

April, 1928
Princeton University

CONTENTS

COLERIDGE'S CONVERSATION POEMS

A young poet whom I love has just left my house and driven away in the soft darkness of a spring night, to the remote cottage in the Delaware valley where he meditates a not thankless Muse. Before he came I was in despair, sitting bewildered with my heaps of notes on Coleridge spread before me, having much to say, but not knowing how to begin. Now it should be easier, for one fire kindleth another, and our talk was of friendship and poetry. Samuel Taylor Coleridge, to those who know him well, exists in three modes, as Philosopher, Poet, Friend. If the truth were told, we should all be obliged to admit that the Philosopher escapes us. We hear his voice and enter the room where he is speaking, only to see his retreating figure down some dim corridor. " Aids to Reflection," " Table Talk," and other echoes of his speech yield merely a confused murmur, baffling, and the more exasperating because the tones are in themselves melodious. It was an unprofitable heritage that Coleridge left to his disciple, Joseph Henry Green, and to his daughter Sara and her husband, the task of arranging and publishing his philosophical writings and the records of his innumerable monologues. In Green's case the labor lasted twenty-eight years. The sum of all this toil is neither a rounded system nor a clear view of anything in particular. They tried earnestly to catch the vanishing metaphysician, but in vain.

It is the opinion of many that Coleridge as Poet is almost equally an evanescent shadow; and though the many are in this quite mistaken, they have some excuse for thinking thus, because his fulfilment falls far short of his promise. But they fail to appreciate how very great, after all, the fulfilment is. The causes of this injustice to Coleridge the Poet are the splendor of the three poems of his which everybody knows and admires, and also the habit of regarding him as a mere satellite of Wordsworth, or at least as Wordsworth's weaker brother. Those who are so dazzled by " The Rime of the Ancient Mariner," " Kubla Khan," and " Christabel," that all the rest of Coleridge's poetry seems to them colorless, are invited to reopen his book, but first to read J. Dykes Campbell's Life of him or the collection of his wonderful letters edited by the late Ernest Hartley Coleridge, his grandson; and I wish to direct the attention of those from whom he is obscured by the greater glory of Wordsworth to a group of poems which can be compared only to the "Lines composed a few miles above Tintern Abbey."

These are his Poems of Friendship. They cannot

be even vaguely understood unless the reader knows what persons Coleridge has in mind. They are, for the most part, poems in which reference is made with fine particularity to certain places. They were composed as the expression of feelings which were occasioned by quite definite events. Between the lines, when we know their meaning, we catch glimpses of those delightful people who formed the golden inner circle of his friends in the days of his young manhood: Charles Lamb, his oldest and dearest, Mary Lamb, practical Tom Poole, William and Dorothy Wordsworth in their days of clearest vision and warmest enthusiasm, and in the later pieces Mrs. Wordsworth and Sarah Hutchinson her young sister. They may all be termed, as Coleridge himself names one or two of them, Conversation Poems, for even when they are soliloquies the sociable man who wrote them could not even think without supposing a listener. They require and reward considerable knowledge of his life and especially the life of his heart.

This is not so certainly the case with his three famous Mystery Poems, in which the spellbound reader sees visions and hears music which float in from a magic realm and float out again into unfathomable space. Their perfection is not of this world nor founded on history or circumstance. No knowledge of their origin or mechanism can increase their beauty or enrich their charm. To attempt to account for them, to write footnotes about them, if it were hoped thereby to make them more powerful in their effect upon the imagination, would be ridiculous and pedantic, however fruitful of knowledge and interest the exercise might be.

While the Philosopher has wandered away into a vague limbo of unfinished projects and the Poet of "Christabel" and its companion stars can only gaze in mute wonder upon the constellation he fixed in the heavens, the Poet of the Friendly Pieces lingers among us and can be questioned. We owe it to him and to ourselves to appreciate them. It is unfair to his genius that he should be represented in most anthologies of English verse only by the Mystery Poems, and that those who read the Poems of Friendship should so generally be ignorant of their meaning. It is unfair to ourselves that we should refuse the companionship of the most open-hearted of men, a generous spirit, willing to reveal to us the riches of his mind, a man whom all can understand and no one can help loving. There is not so much kindness, humor, wisdom, and frankness offered to most of us in the ordinary intercourse of life that we can afford to decline the outstretched hand of Coleridge.

Poetry draws mankind together, breaks down

barriers, relieves loneliness, shows us ourselves in others and others in ourselves. It is the friendly art. It ignores time and space. National, racial, and secular differences fall at its touch, which is the touch of kinship, and when we feel this we laugh shamefacedly at our pretensions, timidities, and reserves. Everything in antiquity is antiquated except its art and especially its poetry. That is scarcely less fresh than when it fell first from living lips. The religion of the ancients is to us superstition, their science childishness, but their poetry is as valid and vital as our own. We appropriate it, and it unites us with our fathers.

> " One precious, tender-hearted scroll
> Of pure Simonides "

shines through the mist more brightly than the Nicomachean Ethics or the Constitution of Athens. What is most enduring in the Old Testament is the humanity revealed here and there in veins of poetry, not only as psalms and prophecies but gleaming out from the historical books. It is the nature of all great poetry to open and bring together the hearts of men. And few poets have so generously given themselves out to us as Coleridge. The gift is rare and wonderful because he was a very good man, even more than because of his marvellous mind. When I say he was good, I mean that he was loving.

However many other kinds of goodness there may be, this is the indispensable element. Some one has been trying to persuade me that artists should abandon themselves wholly to art. If this means that they should dissociate themselves from their fellow men who have the misfortune to be mere ordinary mortals, or should neglect the duties and forgo the pleasures that other people perform and enjoy, it is a heresy at which the Muse of Literary History shrugs her shoulders.

The Poems of Friendship make yet another claim on our attention: they are among the supreme examples of a peculiar kind of poetry. Others not unlike them, though not surpassing them, are Ovid's " Cum subit illius tristissima noctis imago," and several of the Canti of Leopardi. Some passages in Cowper's "Task" resemble them in tone. Poignancy of feeling, intimacy of address, and ease of expression are even more perfectly blended in Coleridge's poems than in any of these.

The compositions which I denominate Poems of Friendship or Conversation Poems are " The Eolian Harp," " Reflections on having left a Place of Retirement," " This Lime-Tree Bower my Prison," " Frost at Midnight," " Fears in Solitude," " The Nightingale," " Dejection," and " To William Wordsworth " (sometimes printed " To a Gentleman "). The list is not complete; there are shorter pieces which might be added; but these are the most substantial and, I think, the best. The qualities common to all the eight are qualities of style no less than of subject. Wordsworth is clearly more entitled than Coleridge to be considered the leader in creating and also in expounding a new kind of poetry, though a careless examination of their early works might lead one to think that they came forward simultaneously and independent of each other as reformers. Until he met Wordsworth, which was probably in 1795, Coleridge wrote in the manner which had been fashionable since the death of Milton, employing without hesitation all those poetic licences which constituted what he later termed " Gaudyverse," in contempt. Wordsworth, on the other hand, though employing the same devices in his first published poems, " An Evening Walk " and " Descriptive Sketches," showed, here and there even in those juvenile compositions, a naturalness which foretold the revolt accomplished in " Guilt and Sorrow," dating from 1794. If one reads Coleridge's early poems in chronological order, one will perceive that Gaudyverse persists till about the middle of 1795, and then quickly yields to the natural style which Wordsworth was practising.

"The Eolian Harp," composed on Aug. 20, 1795, in the short period when Coleridge was happy in his approaching marriage, sounds many a note of the *dolce stil nuovo,* and is moreover in substance his first important and at the same time characteristic poem. The influence of Wordsworth, whose early works he had read, is to be seen in small details, such as a bold and faithful reference to the scents " snatched from yon beanfield." The natural happiness of Coleridge, which was to break forth from him in spite of sorrow through all his darkened later years, flows like a sunlit river in this poem. In two magnificent passages he anticipates by nearly three years the grand climax of the " Lines composed a few miles above Tintern Abbey," singing:

" O! the one Life within us and abroad,
   Which meets all motion and becomes its soul,
   A light in sound, a sound-like power in light,
   Rhythm in all thought, and joyance everywhere —

     .   .   .   .

   And what if all of animated nature
   Be but organic Harps diversely framed,
   That tremble into thought, as o'er them sweeps,
   Plastic and vast, one intellectual breeze,
   At once the Soul of each, and God of all."

Here is the Philosopher at his best, but he steps down from the intellectual throne at the bidding of love; and out of consideration for Sarah's religious scruples, and in obedience to his own deep humility, apologizes for

" These shapings of the unregenerate mind."

It is to be noted also that the blank verse is more fluent and easy than Milton's, or any that had been written since Milton, moving with a gentle yet sufficiently strong rhythm, and almost free from the suggestion of the heroic couplet, a suggestion which is *felt* in nearly all 18th-century unrhymed verse, as of something recently lost and not quite forgotten. The cadences are long and beautiful, binding line to line and sentence to sentence in a way that the constant use of couplets and stanzas had made rare since Milton's time.

A few weeks later Coleridge wrote " Reflections on having left a Place of Retirement." The poem begins with a quiet description of the surrounding scene and, after a superb flight of imagination, brings the mind back to the starting-point, a pleasing device which we may call the " return." The imagination, in the second poem, seeks not, as in the first, a metaphysical, but an ethical height. The poet is tormented in the midst of his happiness by the thought of those who live in wretchedness or who die in the war, and asks himself:

> " Was it right
> While my unnumbered brethren toiled and bled,
> That I should dream away the entrusted hours
> On rose-leaf beds, pampering the coward heart
> With feelings all too delicate for use? "

The problem is not stated in abstract, but in concrete terms. In fact, the only abstract passages in the Conversation Poems are the two quoted above, from " The Eolian Harp "; and in general it is noticeable that Coleridge, whose talk was misty and whose prose writings are often like a cloud, luminous but impossible to see through, is one of the simplest and most familiar of poets. He, the subtlest metaphysician in England, was, as a poet, content to express elementary and universal feelings in the plainest terms.

On July 2, 1797, Coleridge, with Dorothy Wordsworth sitting beside him, drove from Racedown in Dorset to Nether Stowey in Somerset, and for about two weeks the small cottage behind Tom Poole's hospitable mansion sheltered William and Dorothy and perhaps Basil Montague's little boy, whom they were educating, besides Coleridge and Mrs. Coleridge and Hartley the baby and Nanny their maid. To fill up the measure, Charles Lamb joined them on the 7th and stayed a week. Coleridge, writing to Southey, says:

" The second day after Wordsworth came to me, dear Sara accidentally emptied a skillet of boiling milk on my foot, which confined me during the whole time of C. Lamb's stay, and still prevents me from all walks longer than a furlong. While Wordsworth, his sister, and Charles Lamb were out one evening, sitting in the arbour of

T. Poole's garden, which communicates with mine, I composed these lines, with which I am pleased."

He encloses the poem " This Lime-Tree Bower my Prison," in which he refers tenderly to his guests as " my Sister and my Friends." It begins:

> " Well, they are gone, and here I must remain,
>   This lime-tree bower my prison! I have lost
>   Beauties and feelings such as would have been
>   Most sweet to my remembrance even when age
>   Had dimmed mine eyes to blindness! "

In imagination he follows them as they " wander in gladness along the hill-top edge," and thinks with special satisfaction of the pleasure granted to his gentle-hearted Charles, who had been long " in the great City pent," an expression which he uses again in " Frost at Midnight " and which Wordsworth later adopted, both of them echoing a line of Milton. The idea of storing up happy memories for some wintry season of the heart, an idea expanded by Wordsworth in " Tintern Abbey," and again in " I wandered lonely as a Cloud," occurs in the lines quoted above; and Wordsworth's famous brave remark,

> " Nature never did betray
>   The heart that loved her,"

is also anticipated in this poem when Coleridge declares,

> "Henceforth I shall know
> That Nature ne'er deserts the wise and pure,"

the wise and pure, we may be certain, being in their eyes those who love Nature. In this third Conversation Poem Coleridge has risen above the level attained in the former two; Gaudyverse is gone entirely, and unaffected simplicity, the perfection of tranquil ease, reigns without a rival. No better example, even in Wordsworth's own verse, could be found to illustrate the theory set forth three years later in the Preface to "Lyrical Ballads." The beauty and truth of the poem and the picture it gives of Coleridge's yearning heart of love do not depend upon the fact that it was an illustrious trio whom he followed in imagination as they roved " upon smooth Quantock's airy ridge "; it is a clear boon to us that they happened to be no less than Charles Lamb and Dorothy and William Wordsworth. The significant thing is Coleridge's unselfish delight in the joys of others. Happiness of this kind is an inexhaustible treasure to which all have access.

" Frost at Midnight," composed in February, 1798, also dates from that most blessed time, when he was living in concord with his wife, under the wide-branching protection of strong Thomas Poole, with William and Dorothy near and poetry pouring unto him from the heaven's height. It is the mus-

ing of a father beside the cradle of his child, and
the passage is well known in which he foretells that
Hartley shall

> " wander like a breeze
> By lakes and sandy shores, beneath the crags
> Of ancient mountain."

The chief beauty of the poem, however, is in its
" return," which is the best example of the peculiar
kind of blank verse Coleridge had evolved, as natural-seeming as prose, but as exquisitely artistic as
the most complicated sonnet:

> " Therefore all seasons shall be sweet to thee,
> Whether the summer clothe the general earth
> With greenness, or the redbreast sit and sing
> Betwixt the tufts of snow on the bare branch
> Of mossy apple-tree, while the nigh thatch
> Smokes in the sun-thaw; whether the eave-drops fall
> Heard only in the trances of the blast,
> Or if the secret ministry of frost
> Shall hang them up in silent icicles,
> Quietly shining to the quiet Moon."

" Fears in Solitude," written in April 1798,
" during the alarm of an invasion," is the longest of
the Conversation Poems. It begins characteristically
in a low key, with a quiet description of the poet's
surroundings. He is reposing, happy and tranquil,
in a green dell, above which sings a skylark in the
clouds. Then quite suddenly his conscience cries

out, when he thinks, as in " Reflections on having
left a Place of Retirement," of the dangers and sufferings of others. From self-tormenting he passes
into an indictment of his countrymen for going
lightly to war and for having " borne to distant
tribes " slavery, suffering, and vice. In words of
terrible sincerity he charges society and his age
with hardness and frivolity. " We have loved," he
cries, " to swell the war-whoop, passionate for war."
To read of war has become " the best amusement
for our morning meal." We have turned the forms
of holy religion into blasphemy, until

> " the owlet Atheism,
> Sailing on obscene wings athwart the noon,
> Drops his blue-fringèd lids, and holds them close,
> And hooting at the glorious sun in Heaven,
> Cries out ' Where is it? ' "

Down to the 129th line the strain of passionate pa-
cificism continues. It is the confession of a tender-
hearted, conscience-stricken man, to whom has
been revealed a region above partisan and national
views. We feel that if the passage had been de-
claimed to an army before battle, the men would
have broken ranks in horror of their own designs.
Quite unexpectedly, however, the tone changes at
this point, and he bursts into a tirade against the
French, calling upon Englishmen to stand forth and
" repel an impious foe." The violence of the transi-

tion is disconcerting. But anon, with a thrust in each
direction, at the over-sanguine English friends of
the Revolution and at its unreasonable foes, he
sings a glorious pæan to " dear Britain," his " native Isle." Then comes a sweet " return ": he bids
farewell to the soft and silent spot where he has
been reclining; he thinks with joy of his beloved
Stowey and his friend Poole and the lowly cottage
where his babe and his babe's mother dwell in
peace. It was like Coleridge to see both sides of the
problem raised by the war, by all war, and to express both with equal poignancy. Extreme as are
the limits to which his imagination carries him, his
eloquence is vitiated by no sentimentalism or self-
delusion. The dilemma is fairly stated; the distress
is genuine. Were it not for the exquisite frame in
which the fears and questionings are set, were it not
for the sweet opening and the refreshing " return,"
the pain excited by this poem would outweigh our
pleasure in the aptness of its figures and the melody
of its verse. But the frame saves the picture, as the
profound psychological truth of the picture justifies
the beauty of the frame. Coleridge was unaware
how successful he had been, for in a note in one of
his manuscript copies of this superb work of art he
says: " The above is perhaps not Poetry, but rather
a sort of middle thing between Poetry and Oratory,
sermoni propriora. Some parts are, I am conscious,

too tame even for animated prose." These words must have been dictated by humility rather than by critical judgment. He would have made no such deduction had Wordsworth or Lamb written the verses.

In the same productive month, April 1798, he wrote " The Nightingale," which he himself terms a Conversation Poem, though it is neither more nor less conversational than the others of this kind. It was printed five months later in " Lyrical Ballads." Hazlitt, in his account of a visit he made that spring to Nether Stowey, tells of a walk he took with William and Dorothy and Coleridge: " Returning that same evening, I got into a metaphysical argument with Wordsworth, while Coleridge was explaining the different notes of the nightingale to his sister, in which we neither of us succeeded in making ourselves perfectly clear and intelligible." In Dorothy's Alfoxden journal are brief mentions of many a walk by moon or star light with " dear Col." The friendship had ripened fast. " My Friend, and thou, our Sister " are addressed in the poem, and we may be sure the nightingales themselves sang nothing half so sweet to Dorothy's ears as the liquid lines of the music-master. Many little incidents of their walks would crowd her memory in later years as she read them. The " castle huge " mentioned in the poem is a romantic exaggeration for Alfoxden house, and she is the " gentle maid " who dwelt hard by. " Thus Coleridge dreamed of me," might she sigh in her old age, when he had passed into the eternity of his fame and she was lingering by shallower streams of life, *assise auprès du feu, devisant et filant.*

Thus far we have seen Coleridge in his day of strength. If he has written of sorrow, it has been sorrow for suffering mankind; if he has written of sin, it has been the sin of his country. He has been too manly to invent reasons for self-pity. But he is wretched without the companionship of loving friends. In Germany, when separated from the Wordsworths, he sends a wistful call across the frozen wastes of the Lüneburg Heath:

" William, my head and my heart, dear William and dear
    Dorothea!
  You have all in each other; but I am lonely and want
    you! "

And when he ran away from them in Scotland, perhaps to escape their anxious care of his health, he was soon in distress and crying out:

" To be beloved is all I need,
  And whom I love I love indeed."

Prior to his return from Germany, in the summer of 1799, he had not become a slave to opium, though the habit of taking it had been formed. In the next three years the vice grew fixed, his will decayed, he produced less, and fell into depths of remorse. From Dorothy's Grasmere journal it appears unlikely that she or her brother understood the reason for the change which they undoubtedly perceived in him. Love blinded them to the cause, while making them quick to see and lament the effects. She kept a journal for her own eyes alone, and one feels like an intruder when one reads it in print, and sees in it sure signs that she loved with romantic tenderness the visitor who came from time to time over the hills from Keswick, and whose letters she placed in her bosom for safe-keeping, and whose sufferings, as she detected them in his altered countenance, made her weep. The situation was not rendered less delicate by the fact that he was unhappy with his wife; and Dorothy's extraordinary power of self-abnegation must have been strained almost unendurably when she found that the woman for whom Coleridge felt most affection was Sarah Hutchinson. There was something innocent and childlike in all his sympathies and likings and lovings. He never permanently alienated a friend; he never quite broke the tie between himself and his wife; he could, it seems, love without selfishness and be loved without jealousy. Ernest Hartley Coleridge once told me that he was quite sure the

" Asra " of Coleridge's poems was Sarah Hutchinson, and that the poet loved her. Mr. Gordon Wordsworth has told me the same thing. " Sara " in the poems before 1799 refers, of course, to Mrs. Coleridge; after that date to Miss Hutchinson. She was his amanuensis and close companion when he lived, as he did for months at a time, with the Wordsworths at Grasmere. Their hospitality knew no bounds where he was concerned, and their patience with him as he bent more and more under the power of narcotics and stimulants was almost inexhaustible.

In the winter of 1801–1802, the two causes of Coleridge's unhappiness, opium and domestic discord, worked havoc with him and brought him to despair. The wings of poesy were broken, as he realized full well. Meanwhile Wordsworth was in high poetic activity, healthy, forward-looking, and happy. On April 4, 1802, when William and Dorothy were on a visit to Keswick, and could judge for themselves of his misery, he composed, in part at least, the poem " Dejection," which is a confession of his own failure, and one of the saddest of all human utterances. But it is a glorious thing, too, for as the stricken runner sinks in the race he lifts up his head and cheers the friend who strides onward, and this generosity is itself a triumph. On Oct. 4, Wordsworth's wedding day and the seventh anniversary of

Coleridge's marriage, the poem was printed in the
" Morning Post." It is an ode in form only; in con-
tents it is a conversation. It is not an address to Dejection, but to William Wordsworth. As printed in
the newspaper, it purports to be directed to some
one named Edmund; in Coleridge's editions of his
collected works this name is changed to Lady; but
in the three extant early manuscripts the word is
sometimes William and sometimes Wordsworth. In
this sublime and heartrending poem Coleridge
gives expression to an experience of double consciousness. His sense-perceptions are vivid and in
part agreeable; his inner state is faint, blurred, and
unhappy. He sees, but cannot feel. The power of
feeling has been paralysed by chemically induced
excitements of his brain. The seeing power, less dependent upon bodily health, stands aloof, individual, critical, and very mournful. By " seeing " he
means perceiving and judging; by " feeling " he
means that which impels to action. He suffers, but
the pain is dull, and he wishes it were keen, for so
he should awake from lethargy and recover unity
at least. But nothing from outside can restore him.
The sources of the soul's life are within. Even from
the depth of his humiliation and self-loathing he
ventures to rebuke his friend for thinking it can be
otherwise; William, with his belief in the divinity
of Nature, his confidence that all knowledge comes

from sensation, his semi-atheism, as Coleridge had called this philosophy:

> " O William! we receive but what we give,
> And in our life alone does Nature live."

Coleridge never faltered in his conviction that spirit was independent of matter. His unhappy experience deepened his faith in the existence of God, and of his own soul as something detachable from his " body that did him grievous wrong." Yet he had once been a disciple of David Hartley and had, it seems, made a convert of Wordsworth, whose persistence in a semi-materialistic philosophy now alarmed him. In every other respect he venerates him and humbles himself before him. Wordsworth, pure in heart, that is to say, still a child of Nature, and free, has not lost his birthright of joy, which is the life-breath of poetry. But Oh! groans Coleridge, I have lost my gift of song, for each affliction

> " Suspends what Nature gave me at my birth,
> My shaping spirit of Imagination."

His own race prematurely ended, he passes the torch to the survivor:

> " Dear William, friend devoutest of my choice,
> Thus mayst thou ever, evermore rejoice."

Another awful day of remorse and humiliating comparison was approaching. In April, 1804, Coleridge left England for Sicily and Malta, where he sank very low in what had now become an incurable disease, though he subsequently at various times made heroic stands against it, through religious hope, the marvellous energy of an originally strong and joyous nature, and the devotion of one friend after another. While he was distant from his staunch supporters, Poole and Wordsworth, his creative powers, through the exercise of which he might have preserved some degree of self-respect, more nearly failed than at any period of his life. He came back to England in August, 1806, so ashamed that for months he avoided his family and his friends. After many anxious efforts the Wordsworths and good Sarah Hutchinson captured him and kept him with them for several days at an inn in Kendal. Following their advice, he agreed upon a more definite separation from Mrs. Coleridge, to which she, however, would not consent. They had him now within reach, and in January, 1807, he visited them at a farmhouse, on Sir George Beaumont's estate, in which they had been living for several months. Here, one long winter night, Wordsworth began reading to him from the manuscript of " The Prelude," that poem dedicated to him, in which the Growth of a Poet's Mind is narrated. What subject could have been more interesting or more painful to him? On the night when Wordsworth's deep voice

ceased declaiming the firm pentameters, his brother
poet, roused from lethargy, composed in response
his lines " To William Wordsworth." Lingering in
his ear was the graceful tribute which recalled the
glory of his youth, so few years past and yet so completely gone:

> " Thou in bewitching words, with happy heart,
>   Didst chaunt the vision of that Ancient Man,
>   The bright-eyed Mariner, and rueful woes
>   Didst utter of the Lady Christabel."

Coleridge's reply, touching for the gratitude, reverence, and humbleness which it expresses, is remarkable too for the lightning flashes in which it shows
us the course of Wordsworth's life and of his own,
and summarizes " The Prelude." There is even, in
the phrase about a tranquil sea " swelling to the
moon," a reminiscence of a remark made by Dorothy one night years before as they walked by the
Bristol Channel. How her heart must have jumped
when she recognized this touch! The childlike candor of a beautiful spirit shines in the following
lines, in which unconquered goodness and imper-
ishable art unite:

> " Ah! as I listened with a heart forlorn
>   The pulses of my being beat anew:
>   And even as Life returns upon the drowned,
>   Life's joys rekindling roused a throng of pains —
>   Keen pangs of Love, awakening as a babe,

Turbulent, with an outcry in the heart;
And fears self-willed, that shunned the eye of Hope;
And Hope that scarce would know itself from Fear;
Sense of past Youth, and Manhood come in vain,
And Genius given, and Knowledge won in vain."

In the divine economy and equilibrium of the world all things have their uses and every disturbed balance is restored. Genius is *not* given in vain, goodness is never wasted, love comes at last into its own. The misfortunes, nay, even the faults of Coleridge, which were so grievous to him, can be seen now as a purifying discipline. I do not wish to preach a sermon in defence of weakness; but in all justice, not to say charity, let us ask ourselves whether the frailty of this great and essentially good man did not enhance his virtues and make him more lovable. He had no pride except in the achievements of his friends. He distrusted himself, and his dependence on the love and regard of his friends gave them the joy that women feel in caring for helpless babes. He lost at times the sense of his own personality, and found communion with others, with Nature, and with the Divine Spirit. He hated himself for his sins, and was innocent of envy, presumption, self-deception, pretence. He sank in his own opinion, and humility became his crown of glory. His power of feeling failed from excessive use, and he took keen pleasure in the happiness of others. He suffered burning remorse for wasted gifts and opportunities, but never whined about the futility of life. He trifled with his own sensations, but was no sentimentalist. He wandered, athirst and weak, in sandy places, but saw on the horizon a " shady city of palm trees," and pointed the way thither.

EUGÉNIE DE GUÉRIN AND DOROTHY
WORDSWORTH

I

A certain young woman wrote in her diary one March morning:

"He has a nice bright day. It was hard frost in the night. The Robins are singing sweetly. Now for my walk. I *will* be busy. I *will* look well and be well when he comes back to me. O the darling! Here is one of his bitten apples. I can hardly find it in my heart to throw it into the fire."

Another young woman, on a February day, in a different country, many years later, wrote in her diary:

"That you are no longer here seems to me impossible. I keep telling myself you will come back, and yet you are far away, and your shoes, those two empty feet in your bedroom, stand perfectly still. I stare at them and love them."

One would suppose that the man who had left the bitten apple and the man who had worn the shoes were lovers or husbands of the writers; but, in fact, it was a sister in each case who penned these words about an absent brother. Between Dorothy Wordsworth, in the North of England, romancing about her poet brother William, who had gone away for three days to a neighboring village, and Eugénie de Guérin, in the South of France, pining for her poet brother Maurice, who had long been in Paris, there is at least a superficial resemblance. But they were most alike in the height and purity of their characters — a springing height and exquisite purity, which set them apart even from other most delicate and lofty spirits.

Sixty years ago, Matthew Arnold, who was always trying to interest his countrymen in the finer aspects of French life, and to that end kept his eye upon current French criticism, was attracted to the literary remains of Eugénie de Guérin by one of Sainte-Beuve's " Causeries du Lundi." Nothing could be slighter in bulk or, seemingly, in importance than the fragmentary poetry, the letters, and the journal which are all that we have of her writings; yet Sainte-Beuve, who might justly have professed to know the highest and tenderest things recorded by the pens of Frenchwomen, said that the little volume, " Reliquiæ," was filled with sweet and lofty thought, and called its author a rare person.

Her life was brief and obscure. She was born in 1805, of a family rich in a noble name and the possession of an old château at Le Cayla, in Languedoc, but so impoverished that they hid there rather than flourished. She had a brother five years younger than herself, who, after a period of religious and scholastic retirement with Lamennais, in Brittany, had gone to Paris, seeking a channel there for his clear, yet by no means copious, stream of poetic genius. He was her pride and joy, though his prolonged absence from the shelter of home, his experience of unbelief, and the failure of his health caused her to live under the shadow of a hovering distress. From her dim retreat in the mountains of the Cévennes, his existence amid the glare of Paris seemed full of danger to body and soul. She tremblingly felt that his acquaintances there, scholars and literary people, belonged to the "world," and that his ambitions were unhallowed. The contrast between her life, deepening at home and growing ever more quiet there, and his, who had ventured forth into change and temptation, is full of pathos.

Her writings have but two subjects — this brother Maurice, and the religious faith which tortured her with apprehension while he was alive, and supported her through the blankness left by his early death, in 1839. She survived him less than ten years, endeavoring in vain to bring out an edition of his fragments of prose and verse. They have since been published, and her judgment of their quality has been confirmed by the best French critics. I remember the delight with which, in my undergraduate days, I read what I still regard as Arnold's most charming pages — his essays on Maurice and Eugénie de Guérin. With their copious quotations from the journals of brother and sister, they introduced me, as he desired to introduce his readers, to a peculiarly refined and elevated region of French life, — a nook perhaps rather than a region, — such as one could not discover in French fiction, though, as I did not then know, places like it may be found in French memoirs.

Mr. George Saintsbury, in his rough, hurried style, stupidly grumbles: " One may marvel, and almost grow angry at the whim which made Mr. Arnold waste two whole essays on an amiable and interesting person like Eugénie de Guérin and a mere nobody like her brother. They are very pretty essays in themselves. . . . Seventy-two mortal pages of Mr. Arnold's, at his very best time, wasted on a brother and sister who happened to be taken up by Sainte-Beuve! " Mr. Saintsbury continues: " Even in the Guérin pieces, annoyance at the waste of first-rate power on tenth-rate people need not wholly blind us to the grace of the exposition and to the charming eulogy of ' distinction ' at the end."

" The Guérin pieces "! What elegant rhetoric!

" Tenth-rate people "! What discernment, and what amenity!

With no encouragement, then, from Mr. Saintsbury, but heartened by the company of two " strong siding champions," Sainte-Beuve and Arnold, I venture to say that her poor little fragments of writing show Eugénie de Guérin to have been a very distinguished woman, indeed.

Beauty, wisdom, power, distinction, — the rarest of these is distinction. It is a quality, not an attribute, and generally an inherent grace rather than a faculty acquired. It has a negative and a positive element. The negative element is entire freedom from vulgarity; and this freedom consists, to use part of St. James's definition of true religion, in keeping one's self unspotted from the world. One has but to reflect upon this phrase to perceive that it means living true to one's self or to standards recommended by something other than the world's approval. If a man is either attracted or abashed by practices to which he cannot give genuine assent, he is vulgar. Thousands of persons, especially among the lowly, are free from vulgarity. They live boldly, not fearing the opinion of others. They do not seek to rise in any way by affecting to be different from what they are. But distinction is uncommon, because, upon this negative basis of freedom from vulgarity, it requires that an elevated character shall stand; and the elevation must be intellectual as well as moral. In a distinguished character there will be found, on the one hand, unusual knowledge, judgment, or taste, and, on the other, unusual energy, patience, kindness, courage, love of truth, or some other eminent virtue.

That Eugénie de Guérin was one of these rare persons, a few extracts from her journal will suffice to make evident. It will be observed, too, by anyone who is at all well acquainted with French life, that, notwithstanding the obscurity in which her short years were passed and the lonely heights on which her spirit dwelt, she represents much that is peculiar to the French race and much that is inherent in the Catholic ideal. The soul of France, with its possibilities and its limitations, is as roundly epitomized in this quiet young woman as in her celebrated admirer, Madame George Sand, for example, or Madame de Staël, or Madame Roland.

II

As one reads her journal, there rises, foot by foot, a picture of the dilapidated château, with its somewhat pinched and meager housekeeping, its wild surroundings, the domestic servants and farmhands, the dogs and cattle, the visiting priests, the rare passers-by. The touches that compose it fall lightly from her pen and are so rubbed over with religious coloring that it is impossible to pick them out and show them here. She has a very direct and intimate approach to nature, and it is not impossible that she was cheery and helpful and went laughing through the wide, bare rooms, though the journal tells much of tears and yearning. She had few distractions. The monotony of her daily round gave time to note many little details, which would have been overlooked by a woman less simply occupied, and from them she drew lessons which she appropriated with gratitude. The poise of her mind was almost perfect, because her faith was firm. The poise of her feelings was altogether perfect, because her love had one supreme object. Only when her love seemed to be in conflict with her faith was the balance disturbed.

Without being in the least discontented with her domestic duties, in a solitary country-house in which whole days were spent with no more lively incident than a call from some passing beggar, she kept her heart fixed upon the saints and upon God and upon her absent brother. Though keenly perceptive of natural beauty, she would not dwell upon it with frank delight unless in some way she might connect it with religion. Describing her conception of a Christian, she writes to Maurice:

" Through tears or festivals, he journeys onward toward Heaven; his goal is there, and what he encounters on the way cannot turn him aside. Do you suppose that, if I were running to you, a flower in my path or a thorn in my foot would stop me? "

She shrinks from attempting to penetrate the secrets of nature, however much they solicit her imagination. On a moonlit night, when her sister and other girls are singing, laughing, playing beside the brook that flowed beneath her window, she sits alone, writing to her brother:

" I could spend the whole night here, describing what is to be seen and heard in my sweet little room — the things that come and visit me, little insects black as night, little moths spotted and slashed with color, fluttering about my lamp as if they were mad. There is one burning, one flying off, one coming, another returning, and my table is covered with a sort of moving dust. How many inhabitants in so small a space! A word with one of them, a look at one, a question about its family, its life, its country, would lead us off into infinity. I had better say my prayers here at my window, before the infinity of Heaven."

Similarly, she chooses books and avoids books with a view to the salvation of her soul rather than the gratification of curiosity or taste. After long hesitation, she decides to read Hugo's " Notre Dame de Paris," excusing herself for so bold a step by saying: " It is not to acquire knowledge, but to lift my soul that I read; everything is to me a ladder by which to climb to Heaven." She sets down the titles of the volumes in her little library, chiefly books of devotion, sermons, lives of saints, with a few of those poets, notably Racine and Lamartine, who were considered free from worldly taint. This deliberate narrowness in one so sweet and generally so wholesome affects the reader unpleasantly; yet she states but the truth when she laments the pride and vanity of authors.

"Oh! if these illustrious writers had begun with a lesson in humility, they would not have made so many errors or so many books. Pride hatches such a number of books; and just see what fruit they produce, and into how many a maze these mazed men lead us!"

Otherworldliness, or the fear of this world and the planting of one's hopes in a world to come, is not a characteristic of Puritanism only; it is as truly a Catholic trait, not to mention the mystical religions of Asia. We see it in this young girl's account of her feelings on receiving a letter from her brother's intimate friend, the Breton poet La Morvonnais:

"My heart is moved, penetrated, filled, by the letter I received this morning from M. de la Morvonnais: he speaks to me of Marie [his dead wife], of another world, of his sorrows, of you, brother, of death, of all the things I love so much. That is why these letters give me a pleasure which I feared I should feel too keenly, because all pleasure is to be feared."

Not without a faint sense of shame at her own credulity, and yet stubbornly defending herself, she writes:

" I have just hung about my neck a medal of the Holy Virgin, which Louise sent me as a preventive of cholera. It is the medal that they say has performed so many miracles. It is not an article of faith to believe this, but does no harm."

Nothing, perhaps, could do more harm, in the long run, than the indifference to rational evidence of which this remark is an example; but in the presence of so gentle a creature, one shrinks from being censorious. She overflows with approval of the sacrament of confession, not perceiving, or not admitting to herself, that loneliness and a natural feminine instinct to seek the moral support of a masculine mind may have something to do with the confidence she reposes in her confessor. She goes on pilgrimage to " sacred places," though realizing apparently that such conduct *is* superstitious. She is distressed by the free-thinking which has penetrated even the mountain recesses of the Cévennes, and cries out against two gentlemen who find it absurd to fast, to believe in original sin, and to venerate images; and is particularly vexed that some of the illiterate country-folk have been discussing theology. She is opposed to schools, and thinks it enough that the poor should be taught " religion."

It is hard to believe that such ideas were enter-
tained by an educated Frenchwoman in 1837, by a
woman, moreover, whose brother was a disciple of
the liberal theologian Lamennais, and moved in the
literary circles of Paris. Maurice had been one of
the group of earnest seekers who followed the
prophet of a new social order to his retreat at La
Chênaie in Brittany. From Lamennais he learned
that obedience to Jesus means to love our fellow
men, and that this love leads to God and is the essence of religion, no matter how many entangle-
ments the churches may have spun over the simple
though difficult truth, so attractive in our best moments, and so repulsive to our selfish hearts.

How close to each other in spirit, yet how far
apart in rational experience, Eugénie and Maurice
were, can be gathered from one of her appeals to
him on the subject of prayer:

"My dear, I wish I could see you pray like a good child
of God. What would it cost you? You have naturally a
loving soul; and what is prayer but love, a love that flows
out from the soul like water from a fountain? You know
that better than I do. M. de Lamennais has on this subject
said divine things, which must have penetrated your heart
if you heard them, but unfortunately he has said other
things too, which I fear have hindered their good effect.
What a calamity, once more, what a calamity, that you
are under the influence of that erring genius! Poor Maurice, let us think no more about it all."

Apprehensive, reactionary, obscurantist, no doubt she was; yet it is precisely her quiet aloofness, the integrity and unity of her spirit, her detachment from current fashions of thought, that give her the tone of distinction which breathes through the pages of her journal. There is something which, if not admirable, at least strikes us dumb with a sort of amazed respect, in the firmness with which she narrows her mental outlook. She is willing to forgo experience for the sake of faith, to forgo modernness and the sense of solidarity with her own generation, for the sake of beliefs very old and in her opinion venerable — breadth for the sake of height. And that there was not always mere loss in the exchange is shown in many a fine and penetrating remark, such as that " prayer is too often an effort to impose our will upon the will of God," whereas prayer of the right kind is " a submissive desire "; or her sensible statement: " When I feel or see affection growing faint, I hasten to revive it."

No doubt there was a romantic element in her religion; to dwell upon the emotions associated with religious practices, to yield to them freely, to express them beautifully, gave her an æsthetic satisfaction. Perhaps there was moral unsoundness in this; intelligence was subordinated to feeling, and feeling was too often disconnected with action. But her love for her brother Maurice was both sound and romantic. In this love, both reason and will had their full scope; yet it was adorned with all the graces of imagination, hope, and memory. One entry in her journal reads: "I have just spent the night writing to you. Day has supplanted candle-light, and it's not worth while to go to bed. Oh! if father knew!" And next day she adds:

"How quickly, dear, last night flew by, when I was writing to you! Dawn appeared when I thought it was only midnight; yet it was three o'clock, and I had seen many stars cross the sky; for from my table I see the sky, and from time to time I look up and consult it, and it seems that an angel dictates to me."

The old-fashioned simplicity of her life, as well as her constant yearning for Maurice, appears in many a jotting like this: "I was milking a ewe just now. Oh! the good ewe's milk of Le Cayla, and how I wished you could have some!" Slight as are these traces of her character, they contain something unique, a rare fineness, a different tone from that which the world imposes upon its devotees. If they retain any value after the lapse of ninety years, it is because of their distinction and for a reason also which Eugénie herself expressed in a luminous phrase: "Do you care, my dear, for this notebook, in which I wrote two years ago? It is all old now, but *the things of the heart are eternal.*"

III

A woman equally free from the vulgarity which is worldliness, of equally fine moral texture, and of higher intellect, was Dorothy Wordsworth. It is not without a clear purpose that I associate her with Eugénie de Guérin, though at first the connection may seem slight. There is an obvious parallel, and a less obvious but more instructive divergence between them.

Each was born and reared in a remote mountainous region, secluded and primitive. If Mademoiselle de Guérin's family was of ancient nobility, Miss Wordsworth's was what is called in the north country " gentle." Each remained unmarried and poured out upon a brother the love of her whole heart. In each case the brother was a poet, and went through a heart-shaking religious crisis in early manhood. Each of the sisters was endowed with keen powers of observation, which she delighted to exercise; each was aware of a life or soul in nature; each felt the possibility of harmony between humanity and nature, though, as we have seen, Eugénie stood on her guard against acknowledging anything in favor of nature which might appear prejudicial to a religion of otherworldliness. Each was unaffectedly interested in the details of human activity as displayed in simple country life, and

understood the conduct of poor and unedu-
cated people. Each was sensible of the value of
" minute particulars " — a trait more common in
women than in men. Both possessed, though not
in equal measure, the rare literary gift of exact, concise, original, unpretentious, imaginative
expression.

There were, to be sure, differences of degree and
circumstances, especially in the way they were able
to serve their brothers. Dorothy seems to have had
complete confidence in her William, and a belief
that he was almost perfect. After his twenty-fifth
and her twenty-fourth year, they were able to live
together in constant intimacy, having defied their
uncle and guardian, who, for quite plausible reasons, had long refused to let him visit her; and
down to the beginning of old age, she had the happiness of knowing that her care and labors were
contributing to the immortal achievement of a great
poet. There is, therefore, little or no painfulness in
her mention of him, though there are traces of profound anxiety and even acute grief, which she suffered when he determined to marry Mary Hutchinson after, as it would appear, considering himself
for ten years bound to Annette Vallon. Apart from
this, the record of Dorothy Wordsworth's relations
with her beloved William is one of almost perfect
happiness, and I am not aware that biography pre-

sents anything equal to it in this respect. It is a comfort to know that there was such a woman, that there was so full and happy a life; there seems to be some compensation here for humanity's imperfections and sorrows. Of what use are they, if here and there a flower of joy and beauty does not bloom? The foundation of Dorothy Wordsworth's happiness was her confidence in her brother's goodness, grace, and power.

Eugénie, on the other hand, was haunted by the fear that Maurice might lose his soul. Reticence on his part, and perhaps too great importunity on hers, sundered them to some extent in spirit; and his ambition to make his way in a larger field than Languedoc kept him from her through many long months. The record contains more pain than joy. We must remember that to alarm about his spiritual state was added the knowledge that he was suffering from consumption. When Dorothy was only twenty-one, in the terrible crisis when William told her about his entanglement with Annette Vallon, she followed her sympathies and flew to the lovers' relief, took their part, treated Annette as a sister, and acted altogether in a most spontaneous and unconventional way. When Maurice offended against the principles of Le Cayla by turning his back on Catholicism, Eugénie could not stand at his side. Her arms received him when he stumbled home to die;

but she could not look on him and say, " I have seen
of the travail of my soul and am satisfied."

The divergences between the lives of these two
women are very wide, and are significant of much
— of racial difference, of the profound gulf between Protestantism and Catholicism, of the contrast between eighteenth-century rationalism and
the reaction that weighed upon Europe between
1815 and 1848. Dorothy Wordsworth was a daughter of the dawn. The energy of England, the intellectual light of religious freedom, the hopefulness
of the Revolution animate her letters and journals.
She lived in the natural world of human affections,
of reason, of fresh individual perceptions. Eugénie
endeavored to establish contact at all points with
the Catholic past and with a supernatural future,
distrusting reason and her own senses, and standing
upon tradition and external authority in cases of
conflict. Dorothy represents English womanhood,
or, for that matter, the womanhood of her generation of Americans, in its independence, its subor-
dination of merely feminine instincts to those feelings which men and women have in common. What
a man could read and think, she read and thought.
Eugénie represents French womanhood in its full
and constant consciousness of femininity. Dorothy
Wordsworth is Protestant, in that she exercises her
private judgment upon all questions of moral con-

duct. Indeed, her Protestantism is of a very extreme kind, for she seems almost unaware of any corporate religious forms and external religious authorities. She seldom mentions Bible, Church, or Priest. Impossible to think of her going to confession. Ridiculous to think of her wearing a medal to keep off the cholera.

Unlike the evangelical Englishwomen of her day, Dorothy seems little, or not at all, preoccupied with the idea of sin. It is to her and this freedom of hers, no doubt, that her brother refers in the second stanza of his " Ode to Duty "; she was, in his mind, one of those naturally beautiful and good souls who, he hesitatingly imagined, do right by instinct and without moral striving:

" There are who ask not if thine eye
    Be on them; who, in love and truth,
    Where no misgiving is, rely
    Upon the genial sense of youth:
    Glad Hearts! without reproach or blot
    Who do thy work, and know it not:
    Oh! if through confidence misplaced
    They fail, thy saving arms, dread Power! around them
        cast."

As the manuscript was first sent to the printer, the last two lines showed no misgiving; they were:

" May joy be theirs while life shall last,
    And may a genial sense remain when Youth is past."

Dorothy, with her turn for realism and humor, must have disclaimed the perfection implied in the original stanza and have suggested changing the last two lines to the humble prayer they now are. A Christian she truly was, in humility, self-forgetfulness, and love of her fellow creatures; and all the more Christian, it seems to me, because she does not worry about the future of either her body or her soul.

Eugénie, on the other hand, is a Christian in the narrower sense, preoccupied with the ideas of temptation, sin, repentance, penance, forgiveness, divine retribution, and personal immortality. Though beautifully unselfish with respect to her brother, she is religiously self-conscious, not through selfishness, but for conscience' sake; and when she catches herself taking an interest in active life or in nature, she is pathetically startled, as if it were a stolen pleasure.

Shy though she was, and spending her years in privacy, Dorothy Wordsworth sympathized with the Revolutionary movement, which was equalitarian and rationalistic. It is impossible for me to believe that she, with her high powers of intellect, could converse, day after day and through the long watches of many a night, with her brother and Coleridge, two scorned radicals, without consciously sharing, or else violently repudiating, their opin-

ions. That she did not repudiate them is evident;
and I can find nothing to indicate that she gave up
the social and religious heresies of her youth when
her companions sank back into apathy and con-
formity. She was thirty-four years old in 1805,
when Eugénie de Guérin was born, and too settled
in her mental habits and of too intrepid a temper
to be much affected by the reaction which benumbed
the younger generation.

To think of Dorothy Wordsworth as leading a
life of seclusion would be to mistake quietness for
inactivity; for in fact she was intellectually the least
secluded woman in England. While well-bred and
spiritually minded French girls were limited in
their reading to a selection of the French classics
and to books of piety, Dorothy ranged freely
through literature, — English, Italian, French, and
German, — making no distinction on grounds of
mere refinement; devouring the best poetry and fiction her country had produced, from Chaucer to
Scott, including the Elizabethan drama and the
eighteenth-century novel. She was personally acquainted with a host of interesting persons, several
of whom were among the leaders of the age — with
her brothers William, Christopher, and John, with
Coleridge, with Charles Lamb, with Wilberforce,
who is said to have offered her his hand in marriage, with Hazlitt, with Thomas Clarkson, with

John Wilson, with De Quincey, who worshipped her, with Southey, who was her neighbor, with Sir Walter Scott, with Charles Lloyd, with Sir Humphry Davy, Thomas Poole, John Thelwall, and Crabb Robinson; and among friends of her own sex she numbered the lively Jane Pollard, the public-spirited Mrs. Clarkson, Mary Lamb, and her own sister-in-law, Mary Hutchinson, William's wife, and Sarah Hutchinson, whom Coleridge esteemed above all other women.

I think it is quite likely that she was socially the most highly privileged and intellectually the best-educated woman who crossed the divide between the eighteenth and the nineteenth centuries. That she was also the most permanently interesting woman writer of her generation in England, is also my opinion, and perhaps many readers would agree with me if her exquisite journals were more available. They were incorrectly edited by Professor Knight, who guessed wildly, or omitted deliberately, when he could not decipher words and phrases in her handwriting, which is by no means a difficult one; and, underestimating the value of her artless notes, he left out much that he considered trivial or unedifying. A less imperfect edition of Dorothy's Alfoxden and Grasmere Journals has since been published.

Thus the world has access to a gentle power that it can ill afford to lose. We want our daughters to be more fully aware than they are of the life of nature around them; to have a more solid education; to possess their souls in quietness; to understand the poor and humble and be kindly disposed toward them; to be free from vulgarity which is worldliness; to read the best books and write with simplicity and charm; to realize that the highest personal distinction is compatible with the faithful and competent performance of household duties. It might help them to live thus, in the beautiful old-fashioned way, if they had Dorothy Wordsworth's journals at hand, in which to learn how lively and happy and deep and serene a woman's life may be.

I have gone over in my mind all the diaries, autobiographies, and collections of letters I have ever read, without finding one of them more capable of moulding the character of a girl. The educated young women of our time are too well instructed in history and science to be much edified by the timid reflections of the Languedocian recluse; but they would find in the frank maid of rocky Cumberland a helpful sister. She shrank from no truth. She was modern in her outlook, facing the future hopefully. She made a mark for herself in her station where she stood, accepting her brother's maxim, —

"Shine, Poet, in thy place and be content."

And though she could speculate with the philosophers and dream with the reformers, her soul

"The lowliest duties on herself did lay."

DID WORDSWORTH DEFY THE
GUILLOTINE?

Once, at a party in London, Thomas Carlyle, who
had not yet cooled down from the white heat in
which he wrote his " French Revolution," got William Wordsworth into a corner and " set him going." The poet was seventy years old; the historian
forty-five. In one or two previous conversations
they had disagreed sourly, there had been no free
exchange of thoughts, and no liking had sprung up
on either side. On this occasion, however, Carlyle
avoided literary topics and led Wordsworth on to
giving him " account of the notable practicalities
he had seen in life, especially of the notable men."
People were always asking Wordsworth, after he
became famous and old, what he thought of this or
that poet; and between a desire to tell the truth and
an uncomfortable feeling that he was being quizzed,
he usually made a sad exhibition of himself as an
oracle. But of " practicalities " and " notable
men " he had seen full many, and the temptation to
discourse unreservedly about them to the animated
and persuasive Scottish celebrity was too strong to
be resisted. And thus a very remarkable thing hap-

pened: he was taken off his guard and related to
Carlyle an episode of his youth which he had concealed for nearly half a century from all except his
wife, his sister, and perhaps a few other relatives
or intimate friends.

The episode itself was infinitely creditable to
him, a practicality of heroic value, very notable indeed. I mentioned the story some years ago in my
"Life of Wordsworth," calling attention to its
significance while admitting that it seemed scarcely
possible. Since that time I have been at some pains
to learn whether it might not after all be true; and
now the case appears stronger than I at first supposed it could be. There was the chance that Carlyle
might have misunderstood or incorrectly reported
the poet's words; I now feel almost certain that they
were accurately recorded. Carlyle goes on to say:

"He had been in France in the earlier or secondary
stage of the Revolution; had witnessed the struggle of the
Girondins and *Mountain,* in particular the execution of
Gorsas, ' the first *Deputy* sent to the Scaffold '; and testified strongly to the ominous feeling which that event produced in everybody, and of which he himself still seemed
to retain something: ' Where will it *end,* when you have
set an example in *this* kind? ' I knew well about Gorsas;
but had found, in my readings, no trace of the public
emotion his death excited; and perceived now that
Wordsworth might be taken as a true supplement to my
Book, on this small point."

What does this mean? It means that Wordsworth, at the age of twenty-three, with no official connections and little money, when his country was at war with France, had ventured to cross the Channel, had passed through hostile territory, had dared to appear in Paris, and had looked upon that busy instrument of destruction which a breath of suspicion would have caused to fall upon his neck. He must have been bold to the point of foolhardiness to run such a risk. He must have been as resourceful as an Indian scout to come off with his life. He incurred not only the ordinary dangers of a spy; the city to which he found his way was Paris under the Terror.* His action will seem still more like that of a madman when we remember that he had come away from France but nine months before, after a sojourn there of more than a year, during which time he had been closely associated with leaders of the Girondist party who were now proscribed and hunted, Gorsas being the first of them to die under the guillotine. At any moment he too might have been recognized and denounced.

Assuming that Wordsworth really accomplished this perilous adventure, the reason for his conduct is perfectly plain and is adequate to account for it. His love-affair with Annette Vallon and the birth of

* The Reign of Terror began quite definitely on May 31, 1793, and ended with equal suddenness on July 27, 1794.

their child on December 15, 1792, are facts too well known to need recounting. The little Caroline Wordsworth was born at Orleans and baptized there, her father acknowledging her as his daughter in a document duly signed by him and attested by three witnesses. I printed it in my little book, " Wordsworth's French Daughter." He was in Paris at the time, on his way home, " dragged," as he says in " The Prelude," " by a chain of harsh necessity," that is, by lack of money, as he much more frankly states in the manuscript of 1805 as edited by Professor de Selincourt, where the passages reads:

> " Reluctantly to England I returned,
>   Compelled by nothing less than absolute want
>   Of funds for my support, else, well assured
>   That I both was and must be of small worth,
>   No better than an alien in the Land,
>   I doubtless should have made a common cause
>   With some who perished, haply perished too,
>   A poor mistaken and bewildered offering."

His guardians, no doubt, having been informed of his misconduct, had cut off his scanty supplies. He had appealed to his elder brother Richard, in a letter from Blois, and perhaps the subsequent coldness between them grew out of Richard's refusal to help him on this occasion. So intimately was he bound up with the cause of the Girondist faction that he debated with himself whether he should not

remain in France and plunge into the stream of
political life. Though he was only twenty-two, he
might have reflected that many of the deputies were
also very young. Though he would have been penni-
less, he might have flattered himself that he would
find occupation in the turbid whirl of journalism
and pamphleteering. But common sense urged him
to go to London and try to raise enough money to return and bring Annette to England as his wife. So
he left " the fierce Metropolis " before the execution of the king, which occurred on January 21,
1793. What must have been his dismay when France
declared war against England ten days later!

To his desire to make money for carrying out his
plan we may attribute his haste in publishing " Descriptive Sketches " and " An Evening Walk," as
he did immediately, and perhaps with high hopes
of pecuniary profit, though of course the money
returns from such publication were trifling. Little is
known about how he spent his time in London, but
we find him in the early summer engaged as a tutor
or companion by a rich young man, William Calvert. After hovering about Portsmouth for some
time, they parted suddenly, the story, as Dorothy
Wordsworth relates it in a letter to a girl friend, being that the vehicle in which they were travelling
broke down and that her brother proceeded on foot
into Wales. Was he, as M. Legouis suggests, watch-

ing in the neighborhood of Portsmouth for an opportunity to sail to France? And might not Dorothy have been misinformed, perhaps purposely, about an intention of going into Wales? She was living at Forncett, in Norfolk, in the parsonage of her uncle, who had forbidden William to enter the house. Not having enough money to travel herself, she maintained a surreptitious correspondence with Annette. The troubled feelings with which William regarded the preparation of the British fleet off Portsmouth are recorded in the following lines of "The Prelude" in their early form as printed by Mr. de Selincourt from the manuscript of 1805–6:

" Ere yet the Fleet of Britain had gone forth
   On this unworthy service, whereunto
   The unhappy counsel of a few weak Men
   Had doom'd it, I beheld the Vessels lie,
   A brood of gallant Creatures, on the Deep
   I saw them in their rest, a sojourner
   Through a whole month of calm and glassy days,
   In that delightful Island which protects
   Their place of convocation."

The last we hear of him in England or Wales till February, 1794, a period of nearly six months, is in a letter written in August by Dorothy to the same girl friend. It is not improbable that, having learned what his heroic purpose was, the generous Calvert lent or gave him the money to carry it out.

Annette had been begging him to return, writing not like a woman basely abandoned by a seducer, but in full confidence of his good intentions and full expectation that he would carry them out. We know this from one long letter to him and one to Dorothy, both written by Annette at Blois on March 20, 1793. This double epistle was found by Professor Legouis in the archives of the Department of Loir-et-Cher, where it had been stowed away by the police who intercepted it nearly a hundred and thirty years before. It shows not only that Annette had received letters from both William and Dorothy and that up to that time there had been postal communication between the two countries, but also that the subject of his coming over to marry her was under discussion. " I have at last," she says, " received the letter which I was so eagerly awaiting. . . . Its date is nine days old. It is inconceivable how bad the postal service is." . . . " You must by this time have received two letters which I wrote after the date of your last. In them I answer your sister's letter." . . . " I should feel more consoled for your absence if we were married, but I consider it almost impossible that you should expose yourself if there is a war. You would perhaps be taken prisoner." Evidently hostilities were beginning slowly and in a half-hearted way. Other letters got through, even much later. Though the war between

France and England continued unbroken till the spring of 1802, we know from Dorothy's correspondence that he received at least one in 1795 out of half a dozen which Annette despatched, and from her Grasmere Journal that letters came quite frequently in 1801 and 1802. Terrible as was the danger of a journey to France, the motive was compelling. What true man would not have taken his chances?

But considerations of this kind, considerations based on a cloudy fabric of wishes and possibilities, should yield to facts, and we must now examine the evidence. Apart from the general probability that an honorable man such as Wordsworth unquestionably was, prompted by a sensitive, conscientious, high-spirited sister, and drawn by the memory of a decent, intelligent woman whom he had wronged but not betrayed, and by the thought of a child whom he had acknowledged, would spare no effort to make amends for the past and provision for the future, we find the following elements of proof: *first*, Carlyle's anecdote; *second*, the entire lack of anything to show that Wordsworth was in Britain between August, 1793, and February, 1794; third, the military situation in France, which was such, during part at least of those months, that an Englishman might pass through the lines without being molested; *fourth*, the circumstance that many British subjects are known to have resided in Paris and other parts of France during the Terror; *fifth,* certain passages in " The Prelude"; and *sixth,* an anecdote recorded by an honest and intelligent though inconspicuous man of letters named Alaric Watts.

Carlyle's statement is quite explicit. It is vivid itself and stands in a natural relation to what precedes and follows in the " Reminiscences." And although these wonderful pages of portraiture were not finished till 1867, Carlyle's panther-like quickness to seize details and his extraordinary memory must be taken into account. Many a point in history or theology rests upon no stronger testimony. Furthermore, it is true, as he reports Wordsworth to have said, that the execution of Gorsas produced an ominous feeling. The other Girondist deputies, though proscribed, some being in prison and others heading an insurrection against the Jacobins, were still hoping for amnesty or merciful treatment, and they had many friends in Paris. The relentless attitude of Robespierre and his associates towards Gorsas, who was discovered in the city, to which he had returned in disguise from Caen, the center of rebellion, told the other Girondist leaders what they might expect and what actually occurred when twenty of them were beheaded on October 31. Gorsas, both on account of his own importance as a journalist and politician and because he led the way to the scaffold, was of sufficient note to be a distinct figure in Carlyle's mind; and of course if Wordsworth witnessed the bloody deed he would remember only too vividly the scene and the victim and the date.

So far as I am aware, not a scrap of writing exists that was addressed to Wordsworth or written by him between August, 1793, and February, 1794, and though Dorothy in her letter of August 30 to Jane Pollard expresses the hope of seeing him at Christmas, this is the last we hear from her until the next year. I have sought in vain through many a volume of letters, reminiscences, etc., by Wordsworth's contemporaries for any reference to indicate that he was in his own country between the above dates.

The military situation was confused. The armies of the Allies lay upon the northern frontiers of France, and yet there was trade between France and the rest of the world through some of the Hanseatic towns, even in 1794. The Breton royalists in June, 1793, were masters of part of the valley of the Loire. The British navy, not without assistance from French royalists and moderates, was operating in the Mediterranean. On June 2 the Girondist or moderate deputies to the Convention were declared by their enemies, the Jacobins, who ruled in that body, to be in a state of domiciliary arrest. Many of them escaped from Paris to Normandy, making their headquarters at Caen, which became the center of a formidable insurrection against the extremists in Paris. Gorsas was among the leaders at Caen. General Wimpfen, who commanded the Jacobin army in and around Cherbourg, went over to the insurgents and became their military chief. A confederation of three of the departments of Normandy was formed. Military expediency tempted the insurgents in this sea-bound corner of France, crowded as they were by the Jacobin forces on the east, to establish communications with the English. Wimpfen admitted to his fellow insurgents that he had connections in England.* Gorsas, who was a deputy from the Department of Seine-et-Oise, appears to have been particularly obnoxious to the Jacobins, who singled him out in a charge of treason against the Republic on July 28. He was detected hiding in Paris and immediately beheaded, on October 7. Already, on July 13, Charlotte Corday, having left Caen on the first of the month and found means of passing through the loosely drawn lines to Paris, had stabbed Marat. Thus we see that communication, though difficult and perilous, was more or less open, both at the sea-coast and between Normandy and Paris. It was evidently quite possible for a man

* See J. Guadet, 'Les Girondins,' II, 329.

who spoke French fluently, as Wordsworth did, to make his way to the capital. The various accounts of the tragic wanderings of some of the proscribed deputies, all over the west of France, show that they had a long tether and a wide field, though they were nearly all sooner or later captured and killed. From " The Diary of Raoul Hesden," who claims to have been a spy in Paris during the Reign of Terror, a book based on facts, though not what it pretends to be, it is evident that many *émigrés*, who were in less danger than the Girondist deputies, ventured back into France. " I believe it is not uncommon for such men," he says, " to return in disguise, either to give a last regard on the relicks of their former splendour or to fetch away concealed jewels and papers."

Curiously enough, one of the most impressive pieces of evidence that even proscribed persons could move about in France during the Terror is the list of nobles who testified in 1816 to the assistance Annette Vallon had given to them and their friends by hiding them and speeding them on their journeys. Their statement and names have been printed by Professor Legouis in his " William Wordsworth and Annette Vallon."

Christopher Wordsworth, the official biographer, knew a great deal more about his uncle's early life than he permitted himself to tell. Referring to the poet's withdrawal from France in December, 1792, or January, 1793, he says: " If he had remained longer in the French capital he would, in all probability, have fallen a victim among the Brissotins, with whom he was intimately connected, and who were cut off by their rivals, the Jacobins, at the close of the following May." Brissot, who had been much in England and America, was notable for his culture and his philanthropic zeal, even among his fellow Girondists, many of whom were highly educated and disinterested men, and sometimes his name was given to the whole group. Since Wordsworth, then, had been " intimately connected " in the previous year with the chiefs of the rebellion of 1793, he could count upon their assisting him on his way to Paris, whence he would have less trouble in proceeding to Orleans or Blois to rejoin Annette.

Very few persons ever learn a foreign language well enough to pretend with success that it is their native speech, and sooner or later an Englishman in France would have been detected under the Terror when suspicion poisoned all social relations. He might pass a sentinel, but could hardly expect to deceive a hotel-keeper. So we must consider to what extent Englishmen were tolerated. I find that a considerable number of English, in spite of very violent decrees against their remaining in France, did nevertheless remain, enduring a certain amount of

official molestation from time to time and in some
instances imprisonment, but in other instances en-
joying a good deal of freedom. Omitting references
to many English persons earlier in the year, I will
mention the petition presented to the Convention on
October 10, 1793, by Sir Robert Smyth or Smith,
James Hartley, Edward Slater, and Thomas Mar-
shall, protesting against a decree of internment. On
October 16, the Convention ordered that with certain exceptions all foreigners who were subjects of
governments at war with the Republic should be
confined till peace was declared. * But as a similar
order had been issued earlier in the month, it appears that these decrees were not strictly enforced.
Many instances of English people residing in
France and moving about from place to place are
given in a curious book, published in London in
1797, " A Residence in France during the years
1792, 1793, 1794, and 1795; described in a Series
of Letters from an English Lady," though I suspect
that it was in large part composed by its editor,
John Gifford, a notorious anti-revolutionary hack
writer. The poetess, Helen Maria Williams, was in
France before, during, and after the Terror, being
well known as a sympathizer with the Revolution.
When Wordsworth crossed to France in November,

* See Ernest Hamel, 'Précis de l'histoire de la Révolution
française,' p. 393.

1791, he carried a letter of introduction to her, and the belief that she was still at Orleans, whence, however, she had just removed, was no doubt one of his reasons for going there. Her friend, John Hurford Stone, went from France to England in February, 1793, but returned to Paris in the following May. From a little manuscript book by Mrs. John Davy, a sister-in-law of Sir Humphry Davy, entitled " Memories of William Wordsworth," I once copied out a conversation between the poet and Mrs. Davy's mother, in which he seems again to have been taken off his guard, as he was in his talk with Carlyle, for he discoursed about Helen Maria Williams and indulged in reminiscences of the French Revolution.

In " The Prelude " there is, of course, no admission that he returned to France in 1793. Indeed, so far as external facts are concerned, " The Prelude " is not a safe guide even for the year 1792, for the poet deliberately and carefully blends Orleans with Blois and avoids exact statements of time. But in regard to his own emotional life " The Prelude " is extraordinarily minute and trustworthy. There are two passages in the tenth book which are pertinent to the subject of this paper. The first, lines 62 to 93, obviously refers to his brief sojourn in Paris on his way home from Orleans to England at the close of 1792. But the emotions described, the dis-

trust of the fickle city, the fear of massacre, the
sense of lonely helplessness, were not such as he
would have been likely to feel at that time; they
were, on the other hand, precisely what he would
have felt seven or eight months later. In an attic
room of a hotel the young man kept watch at night,
with a burning candle, trying to read, but haunted
with dread, until

> " The place, all hushed and silent as it was,
>   Appeared unfit for the repose of night,
>   Defenceless as a wood where tigers roam."

All careful students of Wordsworth, especially if
they have examined Professor de Selincourt's edition of " The Prelude," know that he frequently
transferred the record of an emotional state to some
other time or place than those which had originally
called it forth. However, I attach less importance to
the above-mentioned passage than to another which
begins at line 397 of Book X and continues to line
415:

> " Most melancholy at that time, O Friend!
>   Were my day-thoughts, — my nights were miserable;
>   Through months, through years, long after the last beat
>   Of those atrocities, the hour of sleep
>   To me came rarely charged with natural gifts,
>   Such ghastly visions had I of despair
>   And tyranny, and implements of death;
>   And innocent victims sinking under fear,

And momentary hope, and worn-out prayer,
Each in his separate cell, or penned in crowds
For sacrifice, and struggling with fond mirth
And levity in dungeons, where the dust
Was laid with tears. Then suddenly the scene
Changed, and the unbroken dream entangled me
In long orations, which I strove to plead
Before unjust tribunals, — with a voice
Labouring, a brain confounded, and a sense,
Death-like, of treacherous desertion, felt
In the last place of refuge — my own soul."

A variant reading given on page 580 of de Selincourt's edition contains phrases which are surely more applicable to the dispersed Girondists than to the prisoners of September:

" such hauntings of distress
And anguish fugitive in woods, in caves
Concealed."

It was by hiding in woods and caves that some of the Girondists escaped capture for a long time, working their way south toward Bordeaux.

The massacres in the prisons in September, 1792, were enough to have occasioned these revulsions in a sensitive mind, but strangely enough Wordsworth, who was at Orleans when they took place, accepted these horrible events as if they were the inevitable, though of course regrettable, by-products of the Revolution, which was in the main so glorious and

so beneficial that they might be overlooked. This
description of his dreams must refer to a later
stage, the Reign of Terror in the strict sense, when
his fellow-idealists, his heroes and former associates, were being dragged from their dungeons to the
guillotine. He probably had no personal acquaintances among the victims of September, 1792, while
among those of October, 1793, were men whose lot
he had recently thought of sharing.

These five elements of evidence, only one of
which is both positive and documentary, but all of
which are congruous with one another, build up a
probability that Wordsworth, anxious to marry
Annette and bring her to England or live with her
in France, left his own country in September, 1793,
landed on the coast of Normandy at some point
where his friends the Girondists were in force,
made his way through the lines of the Jacobin army
to Paris, witnessed there the execution of Gorsas on
October 7, realized from that event the irresistible
power of Robespierre, and was unable to proceed
to Blois, where the Vallon family lived. Annette
Vallon, her two sisters, and her rascally brother
Paul, who was a royalist spy, were themselves in
great danger, for they were engaged in assisting
nobles and royalist priests to escape into Brittany.
If the brave young Englishman had reached Blois
he would only have added to the complications and

perils of Annette's life. The complete victory of Robespierre's party, the extermination of the Girondist leaders, the rout of their followers, and the triumph of the Republican armies over the foreign foes of France, must have made it impossible for him to escape had he delayed longer, and he certainly could not have brought Annette and Caroline with him.

There is one other mention of Wordsworth's being in France at this time. It contains an inaccuracy, which may easily be accounted for, but appears otherwise trustworthy. Alaric Watts, an English man of letters, who was the editor of an Annual Anthology and thus acquainted with most of the literary figures in England between 1825 and 1850, mentions an old Republican named Bailey who said "he had met Wordsworth in Paris, and having warned him that his connexion with the Mountain rendered his situation there at that time perilous, the poet, he said, decamped with great precipitation." The inaccuracy, of course, is in the mention of the Mountain, which was a name for the Jacobin faction, or in the substitution of "connexion with" for "opposition to."

HARDY, HUDSON, HOUSMAN

" Thou shalt be in league with the stones of the field; and the beasts of the field shall be at peace with thee."

Did Eliphaz the Temanite promise too much? Can love for man, can love for righteousness, can love for a supreme law or person ever light up the face of this brute nature out of which we have sprung and from which we have never been detached? The force of gravitation has not, so far as we know, been relaxed to save the life of sage or saint. Fire scorches and water drowns the good and the great, the much beloved and the sorely needed. Is it other than flattery to say to any " awful Power": "Thou dost preserve the stars from wrong "? Is it other than self-deception for a sentient being to say to himself: " They shall bear thee up in their hands, lest thou dash thy foot against a stone "?

From the beginning of human time the heart of man has been educated by Religion and Poetry, equally and often indistinguishably. Twin mothers of " form and fear " are they; twin sisters of consolation, twin daughters of confidence, hope, and glory. A third figure now looms beside these two most ancient guardians of mankind, her feet heavily built, her hands sinewy, and her head indistinctly veiled. She is Science, who has grown with man and been the companion of his childhood; and at last she claims authority equal to that of Poetry and Religion. " We are one indeed," she says.

When Religion had only Poetry as her colleague, it was easy for them to agree upon the lessons: " We must teach the Child through his imagination, using him as the measure of all things; God, we must tell him, is a perfect man." It is not so simple now that Science has taken the third chair. Though her head is veiled and her body is rudely framed, she lifts a voice already magisterial, declaring that there are many things to be accounted for besides man and his projections of himself against the screen of his own ignorance.

What is meant by " supernaturalism " I do not know. Probably there are a number of meanings, some of them gross and some subtle, some of them merely anthropomorphic, merely projections of human ideals, others less naïve. All men, no doubt, wish to think and try to think that an Immanent Will throbs through space and time and life, leaving no cranny of the world of matter unbrightened by Its presence, no impulse of the world of energy uninformed with Its purpose,

"All melodies the echoes of that voice,
    All colors a suffusion from that light."

But wishing is not knowledge; and though it may be that nothing can be understood except on the assumption of an Immanent Will, even this incapacity is a proof, not of the existence of such a power, but simply of our own weakness. And taking for granted the existence of an Immanent Will, three questions turn us pale: Is the Will supreme? Is it conscious? Is it kind? Religion and Poetry eagerly answer Yes. Science, or knowledge based on physical observation and on experience that can be tested by repetition, keeps her head veiled, while her active fingers grope patiently among " demonstrable facts."

A most hopeful sign of the times, in this century, when reasonable hope is so rare and precious, is that Thomas Hardy, our great poet and greatest living novelist, the philosopher who has embodied his philosophy in art which in some respects equals real life as a means of demonstrating the validity of moral law, has throughout his work and increasingly in his more recent poems raised and faced these questions. They had been raised before: by the author of that supreme poem, the Book of Job, by the Greek tragic poets, by Lucretius, by Milton. The reply to Job is characteristically Semitic and accords with the teaching of Islam: " I will answer thee," said Elihu, " that God is greater than man." Milton, the most confident and therefore the happiest of all great poets, satisfies himself that the Will is conscious, but fails to show that it is really supreme or really kind. Shakespeare is forced to cry:

" As flies to wanton boys are we to the gods,
They kill us for their sport."

Hardy's " Dynasts " and the totality of his other poems have two aspects or fields of interest: they raise these religious questions, and they also, under the guiding hand of what we may call science, record the actual life of men and women in time and space, record them imaginatively, which is to say creatively. His novels also serve this double purpose. Many of the poems are condensed novels; the novels are expanded poems. Excepting "The Dynasts," but not excepting every part of it, Hardy's imagination, in all his works, acts upon material furnished by direct observation. It deals with matters known to him personally, contemporaneous, definitely localized. " The Dynasts," a huge epic-drama, unfolds, crisis by crisis, the delirium of the Napoleonic wars, from 1805 to Waterloo. The material was necessarily taken from books and oral tradition, though even here we find that the scrupulous author has visited and studied many of the

places in which his scenes are laid, and that he frequently brings his readers back from the Tuileries
or the Kremlin to listen to the comments of Wessex
folk known to him in his boyhood. Notwithstanding
its enormous range and the magnitude and magnifi-
cence of its chief scenes, " The Dynasts " includes
little things, and here indeed is the reason why it
makes an impression of naturalness. The battles of
Ulm and Leipzig, the burning of Moscow, the coronation at Milan, the sea fight off Trafalgar, can
hardly be called natural events; they were indeed
most unnatural; it was a game of kings, politicians,
and one supremely reckless gambler; the dice were
human bones. But, as in Vachel Lindsay's " Santa-
Fé Trail " the hideous clangor of the brawling
horns is broken by the bird singing of love and life,
eternal youth, dew and glory, love and truth, so
the sweet interludes in " The Dynasts " bring us to
the coolness and health of reality. The greatness of
this epic-drama is manifold; its scope is vast; its
order and proportion are admirable; as an historical pageant it is no less accurate than splendid;
in the rightness of its dealing with mean persons in
their pride of place it satisfies the moral sense; in
describing and transmuting minute details it com-
bines science and imagination as only Dante and
Wordsworth, of all Hardy's predecessors, combined them; and still there remain two elements of
greatness yet unmentioned, one of them Dantesque,

the other unique. The first of these is the power of
hallucination, the power of seeing things with
dreamlike vividness. An Austrian army creeping
" dully along the mid-distance, in the form of detached masses and columns of a whitish cast,"
Hardy startlingly describes in one line:

> " This movement as of molluscs on a leaf."

In a " stage direction " connected with the retreat
from Russia, he writes: " What has floated down
from the sky upon the army is a flake of snow. Then
come another and another, till natural features,
hitherto varied with the tints of autumn, are confounded, and all is phantasmal gray and white. The
caterpillar shape still creeps laboriously nearer,
but instead of increasing in size by the rules of perspective, it gets more attenuated, and there are left
upon the ground behind it minute parts of itself,
which are speedily flaked over and remain as white
pimples by the wayside." This vision of an army
wasting away, and getting horribly *smaller as it
comes nearer*, is like a nightmare, distinct, terrify-
ing, unavoidable. Insight so natural-seeming and
yet so unusual as to be akin to hallucination is
shown in the following lines from a chorus before
the " Waterloo " Act:

> " The mole's tunnelled chambers are crushed by wheels,
>   The larks' eggs scattered, their owners fled;
>   And the hedgehog's household the sapper unseals."

The unique element in " The Dynasts " is its philosophy, which permeates all the incidents, yet without lessening their independent values and the sense of reality which they impart. It is Hardy's attempt not so much to solve as merely to state the problem which for shallower thinkers is no sooner stated than solved when they talk confidently about " the hand of God in history." There used to be, and perhaps there still are, university chairs for teaching the Philosophy of History. The world is full of confident interpreters of prophecy, who can tell the number of the beast; Gog and Magog they understand, and the thousand years, and the white horse; the date of Armageddon is not withheld from them, and the wheels of Ezekiel whirl beautifully in their heads. They, and all of us who will not see because we do not feel, have a ready and easy explanation for sin and misery, for poverty and injustice, for cruelty, for the mad folly of war, and the inexcusable baseness of cruelty. Man, we lightly assume, is being educated; life is a school; God is a well-intentioned headmaster. This explanation fails to account for the natural disappointment of the moles and larks and hedgehogs when their little homes are smashed. It leaves much else unaccounted for. Hardy *knows* too much to be satisfied with a slippery formula. The third instructress, who entered so humbly into the presence of Poetry and Religion,

but has by this time become a very august person-
age indeed, though still concerned with little things
as much as with great things, forbids him to forget
ruined hopes, wasted economies, " white pimples
by the wayside." All explanations based on ignorance of the terrible facts of history being denied
him, insensitiveness to the pain of man or beast being not one of his mental cushions, his natural and
acquired habit being to reason from effect to cause
rather than to assume a cause and then admit only
such effects as please a comfort-loving soul, Hardy
is in a desperate situation when he contemplates
theologically the Napoleonic wars, or for that matter any other tragedy which afflicts a single creature. And it is a desperate situation for every piti-
ful and intelligent person. In the sixteenth and
seventeenth centuries, when some of our strongest
theological conceptions were formulated, sensitive-
ness to the pain of others was probably less widely
diffused among educated people than it is now. Men
and women of culture could sit for hours at an *auto
da fé*, and sleep soundly while actually believing in
eternal torments as part of God's plan of the universe. We may be more sensitive and may have
more troubled slumbers; but the pain is here still,
and we ask, Why? Hardy's philosophy is, on the
one hand, a metaphysic of earnest wonder. His pity
makes him bold. I have seen a timid woman face a

big man who was abusing a horse and ask him Why with a courage born of love. With far greater bravery, though with profound reverence, because so much is hidden and the purpose of pain may be beneficent (and oh, how ardently this is to be hoped), Hardy asks for an explanation. He offers none himself with anything approaching assurance. Not for him is Tennyson's bland confidence in

> " one far-off divine event,
> To which the whole creation moves."

At the most we have the hope expressed in the last choral song in " The Dynasts ":

" But — a stirring thrills the air
  Like to sounds of joyance there
          That the rages
          Of the ages
  Shall be cancelled, and deliverance offered from the
    darts that were,
  Consciousness the Will informing till It fashion all
    things fair."

This is faith reduced to a minimum, but after all it is faith and of the very same substance as all other faith, even the most audacious and inclusive. One might ask Mr. Hardy why, having got over the difficulty of having any faith at all, he could not go farther and be a joyful optimist. To put the matter thus is to throw light upon the nature of

faith, to indicate that faith is not mere hope, is not
blind belief, but the quintessential result of rational conviction, after all. If Mr. Hardy has even
the faintest ray of *faith* in the supremacy, consciousness, and kindness of the Immanent Will, it
must be because experience and observation (which
we have been calling Science, the third instructress)
have kindled that light in him; and if the ray is fee-
ble, it is so because the logical balance between
arguments for and against faith seems to him only
slightly favorable. Even the hoped-for blessedness
of distant future ages would be scanty compensation for the ages that have suffered and are still to
suffer. If anyone is displeased at Mr. Hardy's use
of the neuter pronoun in the Chorus quoted above,
let him reflect that to have used either the masculine
or the feminine would have been begging the question, for the chief metaphysical inquiry in "The
Dynasts" is whether the Immanent Will is conscious, or, to put it in more usual form, whether
God is a person. In his Preface the author says what
is no doubt true of himself, though it may not be as
true of all " thinkers " as he supposes: " The abandonment of the masculine pronoun in allusions to
the First or Fundamental Energy seemed a necessary and logical consequence of the long abandonment by thinkers of the anthropomorphic conception of the same."

Hardy's philosophy, I have ventured to say, is a metaphysic of earnest and, I may add, of distressed wonder. It is also an ethic of pity. The author of " Tess of the D'Urbervilles " and " Jude the Obscure " cannot justly be termed ignorant of human sorrow and its causes. Nor can it be that life's tragedies touch him lightly. His novels and his poems are alike in this, that they were born of the travail of his soul. In the Apology that introduced his volume of " Late Lyrics and Earlier," in 1922, he has with high self-respect proclaimed the ethical purpose of his writings: " Happily there are some who feel . . . that comment on where the world stands is very much the reverse of needless in these disordered years of our prematurely afflicted century: that amendment and not madness lies that way. And looking down the future these few hold fast to the same: that whether the human and kindred animal races survive till the exhaustion or destruction of the globe, or whether these races perish and are succeeded by others before that conclusion comes, pain to all upon it, tongued or dumb, shall be kept down to a minimum by loving-kindness, operating through scientific knowledge." And he protests that what is alleged to be his " pessimism " is in truth only " the exploration of reality and the first step toward the soul's betterment and the body's too." He tells us also, in the same Apology, that he dreams of an alliance, by means of the interfusing effect of poetry, " between religion, which must be retained unless the world is to perish, and complete rationality, which must come, unless also the world is to perish."

All the foregoing remarks about Thomas Hardy have had a restricted scope and a particular purpose. I have tried to show that knowledge, coming through observation and experience, has in his case co-operated to an uncommon degree with poetry and religion as an inspirer of artistic creation; that his knowledge has determined the character of his metaphysical belief, making it small and weak, but highly respectable because thoroughly rational; and finally that in moral practice his strong desire has been to relieve suffering through an unflinching revelation of its causes. I have as yet said nothing about the very thing that makes him a great artist, his immense relish for life. It is a piece of pleasant irony that a man whose metaphysics are so extremely skeptical, and whose ethical impulses lead him to the contemplation of sin and pain, should nevertheless be a joyous lover of beauty. He is one of those fortunate lovers of beauty who are not dependent upon the gala days and splendid hours of their goddess, not likely to be starved by her petulant whims any more than pampered by her indulgence. They know her in her homeliest attire and are with her at all times. It is not the extraordinary alone, either in nature or in humanity, that interests Hardy. He is Wordsworthian in the breadth of his interest in what his master so quaintly called " the goings-on of the universe." All his readers know, or if they do not know they feel, that his descriptions of places are accurate because he has observed in nature the details from which he composes his pictures. Fewer, probably, perceive that these details are nearly always in themselves beautiful and were chosen with affectionate care. This is true also of the traits which Hardy assembles in creating his characters. Even his dangerous, weak, and perverse people are made up of lovable features; and as for his great tragic figures, it is love, not hate, that is their undoing. In fact, the ever-recurring subject in Hardy's poems, even more than in his novels, is the pain that mortals bring upon themselves and one another in consequence of love, and upon this theme he plays in all its varieties, permutations, and degrees. Were he a less enthusiastic admirer of human nature, he would have given more blame to selfishness and less to the antics of mischance. Love, brief in its happiness, long in its disappointment, the loneliness of craving hearts, reverie and the glamour of what is gone, this tragic and yet glorious thing, and one other thing, the deathless beauty of the world, are, it seems to me, the elements of Hardy's art.

Another great writer, whose philosophy was like Hardy's and whose understanding of nature and love of nature were perhaps even deeper than Hardy's, has recently died, leaving a fame which had just begun to grow with leaps and bounds, although at the time he was in his eightieth year. I refer to W. H. Hudson, the author of many books of travel and scientific observation, and of " Far Away and Long Ago," the story of his own boyhood. This is one of those rare and precious pieces of literature upon which the world depends, more than upon any other kind of book, for knowledge of the human heart, a genuine autobiography. It is the record of a wholesome and singularly happy childhood, passed in unusually interesting circumstances, a natural life, untainted with morbidness, and afflicted only with those sorrows that come sooner or later to all. Apart from the information provided in this book, very little is generally known about Hudson's life. But from his numerous other writings it is possible to gather enough supplementary impressions to form a picture of him. Some of the peculiarities which distinguish him from most men are the same as Hardy's. Spending the years of his boyhood on a lonely ranch in Argentina, with haphazard instruction from erratic tutors, he was thrown back upon nature for entertainment and early showed a passionate curiosity about wild life. Human visitors were so infrequent that they too made a deep impression upon him, as if they were rare specimens of natural history. In him were combined the direct and practical observation of an Indian with the scientific interest of a thoughtful, civilized young man; but the field-craft came first and formed the basis. He appears to have accumulated a vast store of information about birds and beasts and plants and weather before he began the systematic study of ornithology or zoölogy or botany or meteorology. It was an ideal education, with no short-cuts, no imposed theories. The best education is self-education, with just enough guidance to save the pupil from a wasteful groping in blind alleys; and such was Hudson's training. It kept his curiosity alive, kept his appreciation of knowledge fresh and keen, gave him at every point a conqueror's joy.

In a very remarkable chapter of " Far Away and Long Ago," entitled " A Boy's Animism," he tells of a deeper and more subtle experience, which few town-bred and school-educated children can have had. In his eighth or ninth year he began to be conscious of something more than a childish delight in nature, a spirit in nature more impressive, more awe-compelling than any of the manifestations of nature themselves. " This faculty or instinct of the dawning mind is or has always seemed to me," he says, " essentially religious in character; undoubt-

edly it is the root of all nature-worship, from fe-
tichism to the highest pantheistic development. It
was more to me in those early days than all the religious instruction I received from my mother."
Similar experiences are recorded by several poets,
notably by Wordsworth. They have had a great
share in some of the most valued peculiarities of
modern poetry. The feeling described by Hudson is
strong in Hardy. Egdon Heath, in " The Return of
the Native," is endowed with a half-conscious life,
not figuratively or symbolically, but in deep seriousness and subtle apprehension of a truth. There
is nothing merely "literary " about this feeling,
either in Hudson's case or in Hardy's. Their relation to nature is the fundamental fact for both of
them, the ground of their interest in life, their happiness, their terrors, their sympathies, their knowledge of things and of men, and finally of their
philosophy or religion. Emerson, with his Puritan
antecedents and background, could distinguish between a " law for thing " and a " law for man."
Not so these children of nature. By Hardy, I suppose, as Hudson avows was the case with himself,
the doctrine of evolution was welcomed because it
furnished a scientific explanation of his personal
feeling that all forms of life were related to one another and that one vital force permeated matter
throughout the entire scale, from rock and tree to

beast and man. With this assurance might each have said to himself indeed: "Thou shalt be in league with the stones of the field; and the beasts of the field shall be at peace with thee." In two of Hudson's books particularly, "A Traveller in Little Things" and "A Shepherd's Life," the barriers between the successive stages of consciousness from low to high forms of existence have been quietly disregarded.

As might have been expected, Hardy and Hudson, being so deeply interested in objects outside of themselves and so devoted to reality, resemble each other in manner of expression. Each writes clearly, simply, and in an original, individual style. Both are so interested in detail, so determined to set forth detail with absolute exactness, that the reader is scarcely aware of the deliberate skill with which every stroke is made to contribute to a general effect. They are alike also in having no easily discoverable political or social theories, no class prejudices, and yet withal having attained an individual philosophy, in which questions are more prominent than answers, a philosophy broadly based upon observation of nature and man, but timid in its conclusions and modest in its claims. What they might have termed supernatural in their own view of the world would by most people be called mere naturalism. No doubt it has failed to supply them with the confident hope of a future personal and conscious existence; but it has given them joy in this life and the material for a sound morality. Surely such a religion is superior to one which saddens this life and perverts the morals of its followers, though giving them full assurance of unending consciousness after death. There are religions of this kind, fanatical forms of Christianity and of Mohammedanism. How remote from a selfish desire for immortality were the joy in nature, the human loving-kindness of Jesus, and his absorption in the common life of his fellowmen, is not enough appreciated, and how inconsistent with some of the theological statements made in his name and some of the aberrations of conduct that have ensued.

Though Hudson is most conspicuously a student of natural history and Hardy a novelist, their works are in essence poetical. And they are both very voluminous writers. Mr. Alfred Edward Housman, a professor of Latin in Cambridge University, a severe classical scholar and critic, sixty-six years old, a genial companion with his intimate friends, a shy and reticent man in larger company, is the author of two little books of short lyrics, " A Shropshire Lad," published in 1896, and " Last Poems," published in 1922. The small number of these compositions, their brevity, the long interval of time between the two volumes, have been often remarked, and also the singularity of the fact that a refined and learned scholar should have written them at all, considering that for the most part they represent the musings of an unlettered country boy whose friends and comrades are careless farmhands, common soldiers, and men in jail waiting to be hanged. It would have been scarcely more surprising to discover in 1787 that the author of the poems published the year before at Kilmarnock was not an Ayrshire rustic after all, but a professor in Edinburgh. And we may say with equal truth that no Shropshire Burns could have harmonized with the vigor and raciness of English song a calm and lucid strain of sadness that has floated down from ancient Greece. While English boys and girls make love and dream of everlasting bliss, a tenor voice from pagan choruses weaves high above their happy tones its pure, undeviating call:

> " The living are the living
> And dead the dead will stay."

Again and again in these two little volumes what seems at first to be a homely rustic lay is changed by a word or a cadence into a wistful echo of Sappho or Catullus. We think we see a village green beside a village church; when a breath of air fingers the leaves of the sturdy English elms, and lo! they

now are " poplars pale " surrounding a broken al-
tar to a forgotten god upon some distant isle in far-
off seas. " Eternal beauty," whispers the wind;
" eternal beauty — and death that naught can
shun."

It is not my purpose to attempt to praise these
poems, more than to express my conviction that for
poetic beauty in the strictest sense of the term,
beauty that in this case depends almost wholly on
sound and on those suggestions, now vague and
again vivid, which are produced by sound, we must
go back to Keats to find an equal quantity of verse
by any one poet which excels them. Even less would
I venture to explain the grounds of this persuasion.
The poems have entered my heart through the
porches of my ears. Among this great artist's cun-
ning devices we find unexpected and strangely suggestive checks in tunes that are flowing smoothly;
deep words, brought from afar, and set like blazing
planets in a Milky Way of simple English; hidden
harmonies, through rhyme and alliteration and cadence, which please like the rippling of unnoticed
rills. There is space to quote only one of the most
effective examples of the consummate technic by
which he suggests far more than he definitely expresses:

> " And then the clock collected in the tower
>   Its strength, and struck."

Mr. F. L. Lucas, in a fine little essay on these poems, quotes very happily Meleager's tribute to the odes of Sappho, saying they are " few, but roses." But, I repeat, it is not my purpose to linger in these pleasant fields gathering flowers of beauty.

What suggested to me the writing of this paper was that I perceived, or thought I perceived, a deep relationship of spirit between Hardy, Hudson, and Housman. They are alike in their keen perceptions, their intense enjoyment of the natural world, and their heroic determination not to let the love of life persuade them that life is other than it is or that death is not its ending. They are not pessimists; their appreciation of good is one of their strongest traits, and gratitude is often on their lips. They are honest and brave. In relation to Mr. Housman even more than to Mr. Hardy, all the common irrelevancies about "pessimism" and "optimism" are more than usually inept. He has expressed, moreover, the very essence of Mr. Hardy's life-work, and of Hudson's too, I think, in the following rugged lines:

> " Therefore, since the world has still
>   Much good, but much less good than ill,
>   And while the sun and moon endure
>   Luck's a chance, but trouble's sure,
>   I'd face it as a wise man would,
>   And train for ill and not for good."

The reader will by this time, I suppose, be able
to conjecture what Mr. Housman means when he
sings:

> " Her strong enchantments failing,
>   Her towers of fear in wreck,
>   Her limbecks dried of poisons
>   And the knife at her neck,
>
>   The Queen of air and darkness
>   Begins to shrill and cry,
> ' O young man, O my slayer,
>   To-morrow you shall die.' "

MATTHEW ARNOLD AND THE ZEITGEIST

One winter afternoon, during my undergraduate days, when fields were dank and ways were mire, I consoled myself for the loss of a walk, " what might be won from the hard season gaining," by reading for the first time Matthew Arnold's " Introduction to Ward's English Poets," which is still the best of our anthologies. The essay was later entitled " The Study of Poetry." No other attempt to get at the secret of poetry and to demonstrate the relative values of poets has ever seemed to me so captivating. It is captivating, because Arnold employs neither the mechanism nor the method of science, but the living organ of taste. It was his literary criticism that most thoroughly took hold of us in those years of the early eighties. He came upon our view in full panoply of learning, experience, prestige, and power. He was widely read in classical literature; and, say what they will or practise what they may, men know that this training is the most solid foundation for a career in English letters. His knowledge of modern European literature was uncommonly broad for those days; and he had done something which in a critic's education is far more important than specializing in recondite matters, he had, namely, by submissive and sympathetic approach worked his way into the very heart of two or three great foreign writers. Look through his works and see how often and with what deference he mentions Goethe, the greatest voice, he calls him, of the century; and note how constantly he keeps his eye upon his own great forerunner and master in the art of criticism, Sainte-Beuve. Arnold's early prose writings are pervaded with a stimulating sense that Sainte-Beuve may see them and perchance approve. It is good for a writer to have in mind one or two readers of the widest experience, the soundest judgment, the severest taste; I need not say how much better than to be thinking about the general public. Another element of his equipment was his pure and wholesome taste in English poetry. This high and sound sense of excellence was bred in him by familiarity with those of our great poets who are the most natural and at the same time the most artistic, with Milton and Wordsworth especially. Wordsworth he knew personally as his father's honored friend and near neighbor, Rydal Mount and Fox How being less than half a mile apart and the two families living on terms of close intimacy and mutual respect. Wordsworth's critical faculty was more constantly exercised in his old age than his imaginative faculty; in literary judgment he was independent, nice, severe; he possessed a keen sense of a poet's responsibility for the ultimate effect of his works upon character and conduct. When the young friend of Wordsworth became the pupil of Sainte-Beuve the lesson was repeated and emphasized, that poetry is a criticism of life.

The spear with which Arnold opened his way was his peculiar method of composition. The originality of this method lay in its extreme simplicity. In every one of his early essays particularly, he uttered and reiterated a single idea, sharpening it into a striking phrase, which he struck repeatedly into the reader's mind. It was his practice also to begin an essay with a more or less unfamiliar quotation and to come back to this again and again for a fresh start. On its ordinary level his style was limpid and swift; at its best it was such prose as only poets write, prose which is thought itself rather than a medium of thought, prose luminous at once and cadenced. Arnold's style, I venture to say, is far more insinuating, far more subtle, than most readers are likely to perceive; by his apparent simplicity he catches us in a net and fastens his opinions upon us before we are aware.

Convinced that a critic so well equipped and possessing a method so reasonable must exercise unfailing tact, I for my part, and thousands with me, yielded too ready an assent to some of his *dicta*. I now think that he over-estimated Byron, and under-estimated Shelley, and failed to appreciate the strength and versatility and passion of Wordsworth, and belittled Burns. Yet so strong is Arnold's enchantment that I can never cease to be conscious that such and such were his judgments and that if there is after all anything like authority in literary criticism he possessed it.

One does not read far in those two precious volumes of " Essays in Criticism " before certain words and phrases begin to leap from the pages: " Disinterestedness "; " Culture "; " A disinterested endeavor to learn and propagate the best that is known and thought in the world "; " Europe may be regarded as being, for intellectual and spiritual purposes, one great confederation, bound to a joint action and working to a common result, and whose members have, for their proper outfit, a knowledge of Greek, Roman, and Eastern antiquity and of one another "; " To have the sense of creative activity is the great happiness and the great proof of being alive, and it is not denied to criticism to have it "; " Poetry is a criticism of life "; " Poetry is the application of ideas to life." They sound innocent enough now, these *dicta*, but every one of them provoked a conflict. And in all these conflicts Arnold's broad views and his large purposes prevailed and spread. He spoke of amenity, and practised it, when he felt so inclined; of urbanity, and was urbane himself, sometimes with mortifying effect on his opponents.

He performed a distinct service in the last two decades of the nineteenth century by helping many persons to resist a tendency to underestimate all values in poetry except purely sensuous effects. The so-called " æsthetic craze," in the eighties, of which Oscar Wilde was the showman, and the so-called " art for art's sake " movement, which derived impetus from the circle of Théophile Gautier in France and was aided so splendidly by Swinburne in England, broke and fell before the higher sense of people who had read Arnold.

I was once asked by his sister, the late Miss Arnold of Fox How, what part of her brother's work I esteemed most, and replied: " His critical writings, his literary and especially his religious criticism." She gave me a sharp glance of disapproval and said: " You are mistaken. He is at his best in his poetry, and by his poetry he will live."

By his poetry he will live, no doubt, and probably longer than by his prose; for it is in the nature of poetry to outlast prose. Except for some Oxford prize verses, his first volume of poetry appeared in 1849. Let us ask ourselves who were the chief English poets between 1848 and 1888, the year of his death. I suppose we should most of us name Tennyson first, and then with considerable agreement though not all in the same order nor with the same emphasis, we should perhaps name Robert Browning and Longfellow and Emerson and Poe and Whitman and Swinburne and Arnold. Among these there are two upon whom the natural gifts of a divine singer were much more sparingly bestowed than upon the rest. In Emerson and Arnold the natural gift for telling a story is not abundant, the natural gift of musical speech is not rich. They are poets by second intention. That they are poets at all is due in large measure to the habitual elevation of their thoughts, their intellectual passion, and their literary culture. Yet they are poets indispensable, we think, in the full chorus, and would be as much missed if they were absent from it as Longfellow or Swinburne. Their place in the entire long roll of English poets is high and peculiar. They are poets of the inner life, of spiritual and elevated inner life. And they present a remarkable contrast to each other: Emerson a poet of spiritual confidence and joy, Arnold a poet of spiritual questioning and resignation; Emerson speaking for puissant and not yet disillusioned young America, Arnold for experienced and somewhat discouraged England.

Strive as he might, Arnold could produce not

much poetry that is objective, not much poetry that is other than expressive of his personal experience; and this experience was intellectual. It is none the less emotional, of course; and it is intellectual emotion passionately felt and poignantly uttered that makes his poetry valuable. The one notable exception is " Sohrab and Rustum," and we may set this noble fragment of epical narrative aside as a *tour de force,* a highly successful, but solitary *tour de force.* His efforts in the dramatic form, " Empedocles " and " Merope," are not so fortunate. He lives, as a poet, rather in " Dover Beach," " The Scholar Gipsy," " Thyrsis," " The Forsaken Merman," " Tristram and Iseult," " Rugby Chapel," which, behind and through whatever sensuous medium or narrative mechanism is employed in presenting them to us, are in reality reverberations of the modern soul and statements of the modern soul's peculiar problems. This is even more plainly the case with his best shorter pieces, like " The Better Part," " Self-dependence," " Morality," and " The Future."

After the music and the constructive art of Tennyson, the vivid dramatic power of Browning, and the joyous universality of Whitman, Arnold's poetry appears limited, hobbled, constrained. But it is nevertheless the genuine voice of a great and earnest soul, whose problems are the concern of all

those who think seriously and desire to see the
thought of their age expressed with candor.

I shall only mention in passing the immense labor of Matthew Arnold as an educational reformer,
his study of French and German schools, his efforts
to secure for the middle and lower classes of England a rational and national school-system, supported and controlled by the state, and by the state
guaranteed against private cupidity, local insignifi-
cance, sectarian narrowness, and popular vulgarity.
In his desire to extend the functions of the state, to
dignify the state, to give organic vitality to the state,
to establish organic unity between the state and the
people, his aims might be called socialistic, though
the instrument of the actions he proposed, the instrument upon which he relied, was aristocracy;
not an aristocracy dependent for its power upon
landed or funded wealth, so much as on character
and intellect; an aristocracy recruited freely and
copiously from the middle class of society. He not
only made these suggestions in books and articles
and official reports, but for many years he slaved
as an inspector of schools, setting examinations and
reading examination papers, one of the most grinding forms of intellectual labor. He devoted thousands of hours to this toil, as is painfully recorded
in his published letters, which give us the picture of
a grimly dutiful public servant catching a train in

the muggy dawn of a winter day and eating a bun at noon at a railway junction between two school inspections, his poetic *aura* laden with particles of scholastic chalk-dust and his critical perception struggling to escape being distorted by the random guesses of bewildered school-children.

The difficulty he foresaw and experienced in attempting to unify and dignify public instruction was that English society as a whole, the English people, lacked unity, and that such dignity as the nation possessed, and it possessed much dignity no doubt, was inherent almost altogether in the upper class. The country was moving rapidly towards democracy; but for a sound and true democracy the necessary condition is an essential equality. Instead of equality Arnold saw in England an upper class devoted to sport and other forms of selfish, stupid, and expensive pleasure, whom he called the Barbarians, a middle class unenlightened, whom he called the Philistines, and a lower class consigned to brutality. A nation so composed would, he thought, in following its course towards democracy, end in nothing short of anarchy; in fact England was already suffering from anarchy or the negation of rational arrangement. It possessed good qualities and good things, however, this chaotic nation: the upper class had a certain sweetness of manner, had " worldly splendor, security, power, and pleasure," had health and wealth and vigor; the middle class had a sense for conduct; but none of these alone, nor all together, could save the nation. Knowledge too was needed, knowledge which gives vision to a people and direction to a state, knowledge of the best that has been said and thought in the world — in one word, *light*. As to the effect of this light upon the Populace, the portion of the English people who had been consigned to mere darkness and brutality, Arnold opened an inspiring prospect: "Culture," he said, "does not try to teach down to the level of inferior classes; it does not try to win them for this or that sect of its own, with ready-made judgments and watchwords. It seeks to do away with classes; to make the best that has been thought and known in the world current everywhere; to make all men live in an atmosphere of sweetness and light, where they may use ideas, as it uses them itself, freely — nourished and not bound by them. This is the *social ideal*; and the men of culture are the true apostles of equality."

These ideas about society Arnold expressed in "Culture and Anarchy," which was published in 1869. He illustrated them further in a volume of lively irony called "Friendship's Garland." His purpose being to excite interest, he carried to an extreme his old method of giving currency to his opinions by inventing and reiterating queer catch-words, so as to engage the attention of his readers by novelty and hold it by sheer annoyance. He went sometimes to the brink of the ridiculous; yet even while sacrificing his dignity and the beauty of his style he is always quite manifestly in earnest. The result of these experiments in angling for attention fully justified his audacity; for the public, whether understanding his general purpose or not, became thoroughly familiar with such expressions as Sweetness and Light, Barbarians, Philistines, Populace, The Best that has been said and thought in the world, Culture, and Conduct.

We must pass quickly over Arnold's labors as a social and political reformer, his labor as a publicist. Suffice it to say that he pleaded constantly for the centralization of the government and the extension of state action, for a sympathetic, a really understanding attitude towards the Irish, for the maintenance of the Church of England as a national organ by which to give dignified and beautiful expression to religious feeling, and for the enlightenment of the middle class, by whose emancipation from the bondage of self-satisfied smugness and unimaginative pettiness he hoped that the regeneration of England would be brought about.

Of Arnold's political papers, I value most highly his great essay "Democracy," which should be read by all who are discouraged by the many and obvious and disappointing shortcomings of democratic institutions, and in their discouragement are tempted to accept a reactionary view. I would also mention his great essay " Equality," which is even bolder and more reassuring to wavering spirits. Whoever may have faltered — and many of my acquaintances are faltering in their faith that humanity is essentially sound and is capable, through liberty and equality, of accomplishing the ends of justice and civilization — whoever have faltered or are faltering, Matthew Arnold stood firm in his democratic faith. And furthermore I would quote with approval the judgment of one of our soundest American critics, Mr. W. C. Brownell, who calls " Friendship's Garland " " a perfect piece of writing, full of the most delicate irony, by turns playful and mordant, and enough in itself to establish his eminence both as a wit and as a satirist." And speaking for myself I would add that the gayety, the semblance of youthful impetuosity, in " Friendship's Garland," were a delightful surprise to me, coming to it with my ear accustomed to the slower and more winding style in most of Arnold's other prose works.

It would not be fair to quote without extensive qualifications some of the hard things Arnold says about his own country. He was English to the core; and an Englishman, if he feels impelled by the reformer's zeal, will criticize England more severely than a Frenchman would venture to criticize France or an American would venture to criticize America: and not only will his remarks be received by his countrymen as the faithful wounds of a friend; they will be praised as public benefits. In England speech is free and prophets are not stoned, though they may be laughed at. How far soever she may be from equality, England is the true land of liberty. This tribute from the land of the Ku Klux and compulsory one-hundred-per-cent patriotism, I lay on England's doorstep.

Miss Arnold made a wry face when I ventured to tell her of the high esteem in which I held her brother's religious writings. Hers was one of the most intelligent and speaking countenances I have ever seen, and there was no possibility of mistaking the meaning of that look. It expressed a feeling which no doubt many of her brother's readers entertain. The feeling is based probably upon one of two opinions. It may be based on an opinion that a mere man of letters had better not have meddled with theology. Or it may be based on an opinion that Arnold's religious writings are on the whole destructive. Both of these opinions are mistaken. Matthew Arnold was much better equipped to treat of theological questions than many professional theologians; his knowledge of the Bible was extraordinary; his reading in the early Christian fathers was wide; he was far better acquainted than most of his clerical and academic contemporaries with the works of the great English divines, with Hooker, with Stillingfleet, with Jeremy Taylor, with Bishop Butler of the " Analogy," with William Paley, with Bishop Wilson; and furthermore he was familiar with the processes and results of comparative historical study as practised on the Continent of Europe. No doubt he would himself have disclaimed being well equipped, for he appreciated what heights and depths and especially what vast breadth of learning a fully prepared theologian should compass. He would, however, have disclaimed being a theologian. Indeed, he would have declared that theology was precisely what he was not dealing with, that his subject was religion. Few will deny that religion is a matter of universal concern, a matter upon which the voice of no man, woman, or child should be denied a hearing, a matter upon which even a mere man of letters may at times have something worth saying.

In regard to the second opinion, namely that Arnold's religious writings are on the whole destructive, one may say that it was clearly not his purpose to impede the work of Christianity. Nothing, however, is so likely to impede Christianity, to hamper and narrow its operation, to divert it from its true aims, to pervert its methods, to limit its application, and retard its triumphant progress in the individual souls of men and in society at large, as a misconception of the Bible. It seemed evident to Matthew Arnold, and to many of his contemporaries between 1870 and 1880, that Christianity was in danger not only of being diminished and distorted everywhere, but of being actually rejected by thousands of serious people who wished to follow its teachings but were repelled by false claims put forward by its defenders. The truth of Christianity was supposed by its defenders to rest upon a number of metaphysical statements about God, and upon certain miracles. To support these metaphysical statements, which were put forward as definitions of God, and upon which the whole structure of theology was built, to support these attempts to define the indefinable, the Bible was used as men accustomed to much reading would never think of using any other body of literature, no effort being made, that is, to distinguish statements of fact from statements of imagination. To support miracles the Biblical accounts were read without historical perspective. But, Arnold thought, it was becoming more and more impossible for educated people to continue misusing the Bible in either of these ways. Serious and educated people, knowing what kind of proof is required to produce conviction in other

fields, in history, for example, or in physical science, were feeling more and more that the influence of Christianity was too precious to be made dependent upon a series of metaphysical statements
which could not be verified or upon accounts of miracles which could not be tested. Hence there came
from him between 1870 and 1877 that remarkable
succession of books, " St. Paul and Protestantism,"
" Literature and Dogma," " God and the Bible,"
" Last Essays on Church and Religion." They have
certain chief and distinguishing motives.

The first of these motives is an endeavor to find
a verifiable basis for religion. What do we know of
God? How do we know anything of God? Where is
the source of knowledge? Or since knowledge of the
truth is authoritative, where is the seat of authority
in religion? The Oxford movement, which welled
up in Arnold's youth and was already, by 1870,
subsiding in a dismal ebb towards Rome, was an
effort to determine whether the seat of authority
was Reason or the Bible or the Church. For what is
universal in Christianity, for what Christianity has
in common with all moral goodness, we must seek
a foundation broader than the Bible, older than the
Church, and less liable to error than human Reason, and this was what Matthew Arnold sought. It
must be something as old as the human race, it must
be present everywhere, it must be capable of be-

ing tested at any time. These requirements are expressed in one word, Experience. " Taste and see that the Lord is good." By experience I do not mean only what is called " the Christian consciousness," but the simple sense of right and wrong that is common to all mankind and has grown with the human race, increasing in strength and delicacy. To love righteousness is to know God, is to know that the Lord he is good. To know that righteousness will in the end prevail is to know that the Lord God omnipotent reigneth, that the Lord our God is eternal. To know and love righteousness is to know God. It is experience by which the reality of God and the nature of God are being daily and everywhere tested and verified. Our only verifiable knowledge about God is that he is the Eternal that makes for righteousness. This is the idea that holds the foremost place in Arnold's defense of Christianity. He states the need of experience when he says: " The license of affirmation about God and his proceedings, in which the religious world indulge, is more and more met by a demand for verification." Experience is the only thing in the world that can be verified. No mere metaphysical proposition can be verified. The very essence and peculiarity of a so-called miracle is that it cannot be verified. The definitions of God with which theologians begin to elaborate their systems are mere metaphysical propositions. They may be true, but they cannot be verified. " The name of God," he says in another place, " is a point in which the religious and the scientific sense may meet, as the least inadequate name for that universal order which the intellect feels after as a law, and the heart feels after as a benefit."

Every occurrence in nature verifies the existence of that universal order which the intellect feels after as a law. The heart too, as Pascal says, has its reasons; it knows and acknowledges what Arnold calls the Eternal not ourselves that makes for right-eousness. All history, all moral experience, veri-fies the reality of this power. Its existence and its influence and its enduringness are daily and hourly tested. It is what we know of God by our hearts. It is the God, not of metaphysics, nor of miracles, but of experience. Arnold, with his profound knowl-edge of the Old Testament, tries to show that this was what the various writers of that age-long ac-cumulation of experience came to mean when they spoke of the Lord, the Eternal, the Righteous One. I am not sure that he does not give them credit for being less anthropomorphic than they really were. It is only in two or three of the later prophets that I, for my part, can discern this high conception. That it was the conception of God which Jesus enter-tained and which he taught, seems to me very likely. In the best authenticated sayings of Jesus there is magnificently little that can be termed metaphysical, and perhaps no reference to God at all except as the Eternal not ourselves that makes for righteousness. He frequently rebuked those who would have persuaded him to test the power of God by performing miracles. His God was not the God of metaphysics, not the God of miracles, but the God of experience.

Thus far I have no difficulty in going hand in hand with Arnold. I agree with him that we have been too prone to make God after our own image, giving him hands and feet, presuming to define him, declaring that he must be this or that and must do thus or thus. The theologians, who are especially inclined to this anthropomorphic excess, which sometimes amounts to blasphemy — as when they speak of God being jealous and angry — have defended themselves by quoting Scripture, and it is precisely such misuse of Scripture that enlightened readers are learning not to make. Enlightened readers are learning to look upon the Bible as the record of the religious experiences of a peculiar people, the first to emerge from the worship of a tribal deity anthropomorphically conceived of, into a more spiritual and universal phase, but not as a unique revelation nor as a volume essentially different in the method of its composition from other primitive literature.

Yet, though agreeing thus far with Arnold and believing that he represented the Zeitgeist or Spirit of Time and only anticipated by a few years the general trend of religious thought, there is a point at which some instinct and my own experience bid me pause. A deep desire remains unsatisfied, the desire to speak to God. I know full well that wishing is not proof, and that even a universal desire gives no perfect assurance that the thing desired is possible. Nevertheless, the longing to speak to God persists. Black desolation falls upon the soul that does not believe it can speak to God. Solitary and disconsolate, it wanders through vague spaces, missing someone, longing for someone. There is no loneliness like to this. We all have felt it. Jesus himself went through this lonely passage, which was in sooth the valley of the shadow of death. Not even the theological prepossessions of the men who wrote the gospels and would fain have depicted him as very God, prevented them from recording the heart-broken, terrified human cry of Jesus in his hour of agony: " My God, my God, why hast thou forsaken me? " And they have left us also that other cry, of perplexed human distress passing into resignation, when Jesus in Gethsemane felt out after God and found him: " O my Father, if it be possible, let this cup pass from me; nevertheless, not as I will, but as thou wilt." We instinctively reach out after God in moments of anguish or fear. We instinctively picture him to ourselves at such times not as the Eternal not ourselves which makes for righteousness, though this he surely is, but as one like ourselves. The greatest joy of which a human being is capable, a joy that lifts the heart and makes it sing like a bird in the morning sunshine, is a sense of communion with God. To miss this joy altogether is not to have lived at all. To have had it and lost it is to be widowed of what made life sweet, is to have our house left unto us desolate, is to forget "The sound of glory ringing in our ears."

I am glad to say there is, after all, something very much like communion with God opened up to us in the second great phase of Arnold's religious teaching, to which I now come. The first phase was his insistence that we can gain knowledge of God through experience, not through metaphysical definitions nor through belief in miracles. The second is his exposition of the method and secret of Jesus. "The end," he tells us, " for which both books were written," — he is referring to "Literature and Dogma" and "God and the Bible" — was "to show the truth and necessity of Christianity, and its power and charm for the heart, mind, and imagination of man, even though the preternatural, which is now its popular sanction, should have to be given up." The power and charm of Christianity, he tells us, are transmitted by the method and secret of Jesus. I must say I do not think these are very happy terms. They require explanation and yet turn out to signify nothing that we did not already know. He means by the method of Jesus the practice which we all know Jesus pursued, the practice of inwardness, getting at the heart of a man directly and changing it. By the secret of Jesus he means self-renouncement, dying unto self and living again in a wider life. He is more original in his use of another phrase, " The sweet reasonableness of Jesus." Though in the early books in which he teaches how Jesus won the world by sweet reasonableness, there are too much bitterness, too much sarcasm and too many personal attacks, Arnold performed a valuable service in calling attention to the fact that Jesus appealed to the reason of his hearers, to their experience, and spoke not in harsh tones of command, but in the sweet accents of sympathy. We say truly that Jesus revealed God. He did so by showing men the treasures in their own hearts, the possibilities of goodness and happiness that lay there, already tested by millions of experiments and needing only to be used. Reason accepts only experience as the test of truth. Jesus appealed to the reason of men by referring them to experience, and he spoke with sweet persuasiveness — he did not strive nor cry.

This is what I understand Arnold to mean by the oft-recurring phrase, " sweet reasonableness."

The manner in these four books is too often insolent and offensive. The method is too often anything but direct; it is too often sinuous and obscure. His defense of the Fourth Gospel as having equal authenticity with the other three and even presenting a more intimate picture of the mind of Jesus, is, I think, a failure. On the other hand, I think he was successful in showing that the true power and charm of Christianity come through Jesus and will continue to come through him when the Zeitgeist has proved even more effective than it has yet been in quietly sapping the traditional supports of Christianity, namely metaphysical definitions and belief in miracles. At a time when he had grown more mellow, in his article on Tolstoi, a more original religious genius than himself, and indeed the greatest religious teacher of modern times, he summed up what may be termed the new theology, though to me it seems the oldest, the original and pure Christianity. He was summing up, I say, the teaching of Tolstoi, but at the end accepted it as his own belief, exclaiming, "Sound and saving doctrine, in my opinion, this." The statement is as follows:

"Moral life is the gift of God, is God, and this true life, this union with God to which we aspire, we reach through Jesus. We reach it through union with Jesus and by adopting his life. This doctrine is proved true for us by the life in God, to be acquired through Jesus, being what our nature feels after and moves to, by the warning of misery if we are severed from it, the sanction of happiness if we find it."

It has been extremely difficult to reduce to a summary the activities of a man who was so many things at once — literary critic, poet, educational reformer, political and social critic, religious teacher. It is nearly forty years since he died. How much of him survives? Much, I think. His poetry has stood the test of being at one time perhaps over-admired because of its melancholy tone, a kind of admiration which can scarcely be regarded as propitious, and of coming in competition with the lighter, more musical verse of Swinburne, and of meeting now a generation of young people who affect an air of superiority to what they call Victorianism. It has stood these tests. Dozens of Arnold's lines are now part of the intellectual possession of all even moderately well read people. Several of his poems have reached safety, so to speak, being already used as classics, in the enormously ramified school-life of the English world, and garnered in all the general anthologies. I think a very high proportion of his poetry, as compared with Tennyson's or Longfellow's or Swinburne's, has passed the danger-line of speedy oblivion. His prose is undoubtedly much less read than it was forty years ago. A certain part of it, however, is still vital, namely his literary criticism, of which the soundness, sanity, independence, charm, and beauty have rarely been surpassed. His other prose writings are eminently worth reading, are still read by many discriminating people, and yet are probably passing out of the general consciousness into a dignified retirement such as that which the works of his beloved Bishops Butler and Wilson enjoy. But their effect, the effect of his educational, political, social, and religious criticism, has been and is and will continue to be very great, greater already, in the retrospect, than the total effect Carlyle has produced, equalled only by the dynamic effect of Ruskin and that of Emerson. In spite of the reactionary movement that has swept over the world since the war, the power of superstition, of a narrow and unenlightened literalism in religion, is weaker than it was in Arnold's day, and much of the credit for the change should go to him. Slightly altering a phrase of Sainte-Beuve's, I may say that in exercising his prophetic function he was doing the work of a poet, for " poets alone have these instincts, like birds of passage which marvellously foretell the approach of the seasons."

MYCENAE

Let not the modest reader who makes no pretense of classical learning turn aside from this article because of its title. We, too, are unlearned in Greek archæology, and are writing far from books, without even Baedeker to supply us with dates and other facts beyond the range of our own personal experience. We propose to set down in the simplest manner possible some things we saw and heard, not things read about.

Ignorance of a certain kind has the advantage that it leaves the eye and ear free to receive direct impressions. This was our case in respect to Greece as a whole, for we went there somewhat unexpectedly; and it was particularly true of a little trip to Mycenae, for which we were even less prepared. The reader who is equally unprovided with book knowledge may, therefore, without fear of being deceived, imagine himself a third in our company, on the 14th of March, 1924.

Greece has been so impoverished by war that her railroads are in bad condition, and coal is scarce; so that there are few trains and these very slow. To get to Mycenae we had to leave Athens in the darkness before dawn and spend five and a half hours in travelling about eighty miles. Quite pleasant, however, was this dawdling along through country magnificent in outline and winsome in detail. We had our choice at every point between views of snow-clad mountains and blue seas, on the one hand, and little pastoral scenes, on the other; between the grandeur of famous peaks and bays, and the prettiness of spring flowers and shepherdesses and young lambs and children, which the slowness of our motion permitted us to enjoy as if we were on foot. The landscape became wilder, the little farms more widely scattered, the vegetation less luxuriant, as the train puffed painfully up from Corinth into a rude mountainous district, following a torrent towards its source. We were wondering if it were not unlikely that a city so celebrated as Mycenae could be situated, even in a ruinous condition, upon a line so rustic and so remote from the traffic of the world. Considering the matter from another point of view and knowing Mycenae had been dead for many centuries, it appeared preposterous that we should find that renowned name painted on the gable of a prim modern railway station. But we did so find it, precisely at noon. We had been assured at Athens and at Corinth, and by so many people that the statement had assumed remarkable importance in our minds, that the station-master at Mycenae was a great linguist. He was the only adult in sight, a kind-looking, elderly person, with all the marks of a railroad man upon him, and it is true that he spoke French. When we looked for our suit-cases, which we intended to put in his charge, we saw three little girls tugging at them in pure hospitality and eagerness to be useful. Our reproof to them for trying to lift the heavy bags was met with bashful smiles; the bones of contention were locked up in the waiting-room, and we turned to the linguist for directions.

"Your train back to Corinth leaves at four o'clock," he said; "the village of Mycenae lies yonder, a mile from here; the ruins are just beyond it; there is a guardian there, who will let you in and explain things." And off we trudged, towards the village, whose white-walled and brown-roofed houses, surrounded by olive trees, were visible against the flank of a bare gray mountain. From the station to the village ran an unfenced lane between pastures bright with grass and flowers. After the tumult of Athens, which, like other Mediterranean cities, is full of strident clangor, we were grateful for the quiet of the fields and soon began to notice with pleasure the little noises of the country, the bleating of a distant lamb, the patter of a goat's feet as it crossed our path, the spring song of birds. The little girls and an older sister of one of them, each clasping the daily newspaper which she had come to the station to fetch home, walked in silence beside and behind us, smiling responsive to our smiles, and all engaged in studying our foreign costume. Their faces were very beautiful, the outlines pure and soft, the eyes gentle, the cheeks fresh. We wished to talk with them, but could not. We wished to show the affection which had blossomed in our hearts by giving them some little picture or trinket or toy, but had nothing of the sort with us. We felt that it would be wrong to offer them money. They might reject it, or, in the less improbable event of their accepting it, we should be guilty of a piece of corruption which the sight of so many children begging in Algiers and Palermo had made abhorrent. We passed a shepherdess engaged in the task, much more difficult than one would suppose it could be, of keeping three sheep and two goats from straying into a patch of young wheat.

Then, at the entrance to the village, our little friends, after gracefully bowing to us, turned aside, and we saw a young man digging in a garden. We hailed him in that mixture of English, French, Italian, and modern Greek which in our helplessness came to our lips whenever we opened them to address a stranger; and he shouted back in perfect English that he would join us in a moment. " I am the official guide," he said, when he came out upon the road. " I keep the key to the enclosure where the ruins are. Wait for me at the inn, the house with red walls up the road there, and I will put on my coat and bring the key." Approaching the red-walled building, we caught sight of the name painted upon it in large letters, La Belle Hélène de Menelaos. The young men from Princeton University who were staying at the American School of Classical Studies in Athens had told us of this modest hostelry with so beautiful a name, and of its clean rooms, and honest people. We entered it with a sense of being among friends and should have been so, we feel sure, had we remained long enough to become acquainted with the kindly, intelligent, and extremely handsome family, apparently a mother and her son and daughter, who gave us welcome to a vast room that occupied almost the whole of the lower story. It was about sixty feet long by twenty-five wide. The floor at one end was raised as if to accommodate beds and be curtained off, and the rest of the capacious apartment served as hall, dining-room, and café. We were fascinated and immediately began to speculate about spending a week there. But we knew, or thought at least, that we should rather push on to Patras, in order to see Olympia and catch a steamer for Brindisi. Many a time have we regretted this unnecessary haste. Travellers in unknown lands should hold themselves free to change their plans for a whim or a passion. All the great and fine things have not been discovered. The foot-free, who have the good sense to go without trunks, are almost sure to make lucky finds in a country like Greece. Perhaps, had we stayed a week in that simple guest-house, we might have been awakened in the moonlit night by the gleam of the whitest feet and the glow of the loveliest face that ever were seen in Greece, —

> " the face that launched a thousand ships
> And burnt the topless towers of Ilium,"

the feet that kings followed to undying deaths; and la belle Hélène de Menelaos might have stolen past the walls that bear her immortal name, seeking the palace that is no more and refuge there with her husband's brother, could he forget her sin and his own woeful doom. We were foolish not to stay.

When our handsome guide appeared we went with him up the road. It ascended sharply towards the summit of a conical peak which stood detached from the range of mountains behind it. They all rose stark and without foothills from the level floor of the valley, and had an exceedingly bleak and grim aspect, being almost denuded of trees and verdure. The peak commands not only the plain, but a pass in the background, and gives a clear view of the sea and the port of Nauplia in the distance. This was indeed a place well chosen for observation and defense in the time of tribal warfare, four thousand years ago.

" Just what was Mycenae of old? " we asked our guide.

" It was a walled city," he answered, " built on the upper slopes of this peak. The oldest part, the citadel and the palace of the kings or chiefs, crowned the very summit, but we find traces of many buildings quite far down the sides. And especially tombs have been found here by Mr. Wace, who has been excavating for three seasons now. When he drives an iron rod into the ground and it is not stopped by rocks, he digs and sometimes comes to a vein of soft earth which has filled the long passage to a beehive-shaped tomb, all buried in the side of the mountain. Here we are now, at the best of them, the tomb of Agamemnon."

A long slit, about twenty feet wide, in the hillside, led to a doorway about eight feet wide and eighteen feet high, with massive jambs of stone crossed by an immense single block as a lintel. Beyond was a cavern shaped like one of those old-fashioned straw beehives that are occasionally seen still, in America as in Europe. It looked fifty feet from floor to apex and at least as large in diameter at the bottom. For how many centuries this vast sepulchre had lain covered from the sight of man,

we shall not pretend to say. "The Turks pastured
sheep above it," remarked our guide, "and never
suspected what riches lay beneath." Riches indeed!
for we had seen, in the National Museum at Athens,
many gold cups and bracelets and other ornaments,
and heaps of gold-leaf, all as bright as if smelted
and hammered this very year, and all brought from
the tomb of Agamemnon, King of Men. There, too,
is deposited an oblong mass of earth and bones —
his bones, unless the archæologists greatly err —
which were found here. And who was he, and when
did he live? Let Homer answer our first question,
remembering that to the blind poet who lived perhaps twelve hundred years before our era, the Tro-
jan War and its heroes were already mythical, half
lost in dim antiquity. And let our guide be respon-
sible for the more definite statement that the body
of Agamemnon was laid with regal pomp in this
dark chamber in the sixteenth or seventeenth century before Christ, more than a millennium therefore before the Parthenon rose like a stately grove
upon the Acropolis of Athens. We dare not repeat
with assurance the figures he mentioned, but certain it is that modern engineering skill would be
severely taxed to lift and lay in place that enormous
lintel and to concentrate the courses of stone, each
overlapping the one below it till the circular walls
converge to a point.

We tried to estimate the age of Mycenae by measurements more significant than mere figures, which after a certain point cease to impress. The result was overwhelming: relics of human handiwork, a city, a fortress, a palace, a civilization that lay nearly as far in time behind St. Paul when he spoke of Mars' Hill and visited Corinth as he lies now behind us. We tried to think back by slow stages, through the discovery of America, the Norman Conquest, the fall of Rome, the birth of Christ, the death of Socrates, — and then to the abandonment of Mycenae, and still further, by how many centuries no one knows, to its first settlement. It was evidently a highly organized society that occupied this mountain summit, not a tribe of nomads, who come at nightfall and depart at dawn, leaving no trace. Traces! the peak was covered and honey combed with them, traces so deep, so ponderous, that they will remain there, in spite of earthquakes and erosion, when mayhap every building now standing in New York and Chicago will have crumbled into indistinguishable dust.

After these oppressive thoughts the present seemed unreal and trivial; and it was with an effort that we remembered the living man at our side and paid attention to his words. " I have a son named Agamemnon," said he, as we emerged into daylight. "His elder brother is Demetrios, and their little sister is Ekaterina."

"And your name, what is it?"

"Aristoteles," he replied, evidently prepared to see our joy in these revivals or survivals of old fame. His English was not only fairly correct and fluent, but spoken with a certain elegance of choice and enunciation. He had learned it from educated Englishmen with whom he had served for three and a half years in the British army at Saloniki, and from Professor Wace, whom he continually quoted and for whom he cherished deep and affectionate respect.

From the memory of pictures we recognized the Lion Gate, through which Aristoteles conducted us, and as we passed the guard of those great stone beasts, much worn by their long vigil, we thought of the captives they had glared upon. Their faces are much worn away, like St. Peter's bronze toe at Rome, with caresses softer than the kisses of superstitious peasants; wind and rain have blunted their outlines and softened the terror of their gaze. The city gates have been borne off by stronger hands than Samson's, though the sockets of the bolts and the watchmen's room in the wall and the mark of feet and wheels in the pavement are still visible.

The great drawback in Greece is the dryness of the climate, which causes a dreadful scarcity of water. We were pleased, therefore, to find a spring gushing from the rocks beside our path as we ascended from the tomb to the citadel. Upon these living waters the existence of Mycenae must have depended in times of war and siege. There was another spring still higher, to which an underground passage led from the inner parts of the fortress. Of this upper town much remains, — an immense curtain of masonry composed of polygonal blocks fitted together cunningly without mortar; floors of rooms; sockets of doors and bases of pillars; and a cistern of vast dimensions so well cemented that it still holds water. By the time we had reached the summit, which Aristoteles declared was the site of the royal palace, we were hundreds of feet above the plain, and the advantage of the situation from a military point of view was very apparent. Professional guides are so likely to be contradicted and corrected by experts to whom they unsuspectingly attempt to impart knowledge, that most of them come at last to speak with caution. Moreover, Aristoteles was naturally a gentleman and uncommonly intelligent. So we shall be the last persons in the world to cast doubt upon the accuracy of his dramatic account of the crime that stained the palace floor and doomed the line of Pelops, and called the earthquake to lay low these pillared halls and make a desert of that city.

"Here was the King's bedchamber," he said. "Look what a view he had over his towers and his town and his realm. Here, adjoining, was his bathroom. You can see the runlets for the water, and the sockets of the door-frame. Next to it was the bathroom of Klytæmnestra the Queen. There, hidden beside her, Egistheus stood, grasping his battle-axe. And as Agamemnon, suspecting no evil, stepped forth refreshed from his bath, draped in a sheet to protect his wet body from the wind that still howls about this mountain, the murderer smote him from behind, splitting his skull. It was long ago, and it was avenged; but none would care to sleep here, even under the sun at noon. They say that la belle Hélène de Menelaos comes wailing here at night, begging forgiveness for her sin and for the woeful dooms spattered like blood-drops here and at Sparta and Ithaka and in many an isle and many a harbor all the way from ruined Troy."

We mused over these things while descending the mountain and did not quite throw aside a sense of "old unhappy far-off things" until we sat drinking a parting cup of black coffee with Aristoteles at the inn, where, alas, we did not spend a week nor yet a single hour, but hastened on to catch the four o'clock train for the fortieth century (Mycenaean time).

MARS' HILL AND THE PARTHENON

Imagine two young travellers gaining their first view of Athens. Both are thoroughly and perhaps typically American, in that their knowledge is vague, their ideas about history and art are not coördinated, their ethical sense is more highly developed than their æsthetic judgment, and they are apt to think in terms of public utility, while strongly craving individual distinction. One of them, Keith, is an idealist. Though by nature fitted to enjoy the triumphs of art, he is troubled about many things: he wonders whether the culture of a few has not been acquired at the expense of the many. He is, or imagines himself to be, a perfect democrat. Yet his opinions regarding society are in a state of more unstable equilibrium than he supposes. His companion, Barlow, is at once bolder and more conventional. He has accepted some of the hard and cruel-looking results of human experience and fancies himself a realist. In the course of a week they made, without connivance with each other, the following entries in their diaries. These naïve outpourings reveal states of mind in which the old American optimism and certitude are curiously overlaid with a new disposition to question all things. Conscience and culture seem to be at odds with one another. The general effect is of a boyish honesty that should encourage us.

KEITH'S DIARY. — Athens, March 3, 1924:

Travelling in Europe for the purpose of culture is a cruel art. You turn your back upon all your home duties, and at the door to every shrine of beauty in the Old World you have to step over the crouching form of a beggar. To behold with enjoyment the representations of youth and health with which Phidias and Praxiteles enriched humanity you must close your eyes to unmistakable misery lying blind and crippled, cold and hungry, on the stairs. Putting the matter more definitely, here are Barlow and I, spending a holiday in Greece, after filling our minds with as much of ancient Greek literature and history as they would hold, and coming with scarcely a thought of anything later than the second century B.C.; and to our surprise, almost, we find here a living people, if suffering be a sign of life. The Athens of our dream is here too, no doubt, and we shall try to find it; but the present reality forces itself upon us first. What are its features? A suddenly overgrown modern city, too poor to pave its streets and suffocated with dust, a population discouraged by a crushing defeat in war, gloomy, heavy-faced, without enough work to keep it half busy; and added to this, an enormous number of destitute refugees from Asia Minor. Ambition to become an up-to-date industrial country, with an army and a navy, has ruined, temporarily at least, a people who were scarcely a nation, a peasant people, adapted to agriculture and fortunate had they known wherein their happiness really lay. *O fortunatos nimium, sua si bona norint, agricolas!* Their German kings served them ill; their allies served them worse; the Turks drove them like chaff; and they themselves appear to have small appreciation of the one outstanding man among them, Venizélos. I counted twenty-seven bullet holes in the front of his house this morning, souvenirs of the old monarchists, and he is said to be on the point of leaving Athens because he despairs of the new politicians. For consolation in their unhappy state the Greeks have a singular toy. It is worth considering, this toy and its use. At least one man in five whom we see strolling along the streets or sitting at little tables drinking water and sometimes sipping coffee from tiny cups holds in his hand a string of beads, — conversation beads I believe they are called. At first I supposed these were "religious" persons, but soon I observed that they were of all ages and classes, and upon inquiry I was informed that they carried these toys in order to keep their minds occupied! Imagine Socrates meeting a modern Athenian thus employed. " O great grandson of Pheidippides, knowest thou what the mind is? " would be neither his first question nor his last; it would stand somewhere about the middle of the dialogue, and the end would not be pleasant for the twirler of beads.

BARLOW'S DIARY. — Athens, March 4:

I have never had an hour of deeper satisfaction than the hour we spent at sunset on the Acropolis last evening. We stood upon the floor of the Parthenon and looked westward through that grove of stately Doric columns out to the blue sea and Salamis and the indented coast of the Peloponnese, and then turning from right to left swept the horizon of mountains with memorable names, Hymettus noted for its honey, Pentelicus where the marble was quarried to build these temples, Parnes sprinkled with snow — all turning purple in the clear light, — and the Pass of Daphne, through which the Sacred Way still runs to Eleusis. Below streamed the city about the foot of the great rock, its houses white, yellow, and pale red; and as the sunshine faded there flashed upon our minds the meaning of the phrase, " the city of the violet wreath." The circle was complete, a garland of tender, quivering colors, from faintest lavender to deepest blue. We shall go often to the Acropolis; there are many things to see and study there; the ground is strewn with fragments of exquisite stone-carving, a wealth of invention and fine workmanship unequalled in any other place in the whole world, no doubt; a designer could find endless instruction in copying them. But its four great architectural monuments are in their general effect quite simple and can be enjoyed in the first hour. Keith was in ecstasy. He forgot modern Greece and her woes and his own tormenting idealism. I say the world was made to be enjoyed; and even from a purely moral and practical point of view beauty has its uses. It elevates the mind and gives us some idea of the eternal. At all events there is something in the thought that twenty-four centuries have reflected the Parthenon and its neighboring temples. It was a peculiarly *pure* joy to stand there. We know so little about ancient Greek religion and private life that we can contemplate these relics simply as works of art, without prejudice for or against the purposes they originally served. They are among the most perfect results of men's efforts to express in visible shape their conceptions of what is noble. So far as I am aware, these columns and architraves were not symbolical; neither were they primarily utilitarian; they were lifted up to satisfy a craving for structural creation, a desire to see large masses

of white marble arranged according to a human
ideal, not quite like anything in nature, though in
all parts suggestive of natural objects and freely
imitative of nature in many details. In how far the
builders were definitely inspired by hopes and fears
of a strictly religious character, I do not know; I
am an unsophisticated traveller. I strongly incline
to think that the vital impulse here was not religious, in any so narrow sense of the word that it
can be defined in terms of hope and fear, but rather
was naïvely constructive and artistic, like the impulse of an imaginative child playing with blocks.
My ignorance has this advantage, that it permits me
to speculate freely about such subjects. I guess I'm
a pretty good American, ignorant of art, but curious and teachable, and therefore capable of being
saved, if culture ever does save.

KEITH'S DIARY. — Athens, March 6:

The nobility of the Parthenon is what impresses
me most; and when I ask myself what I mean by
" nobility " in architecture the answer I get is
" beauty presented in simplicity." " Beauty " itself
is a word that needs defining, but I shrink from the
attempt. Then, no doubt, nobility involves a goodly
degree of size also. There is nothing ugly, no, not
the slightest detail, in the Parthenon or in any other
example of ancient Greek art that we have yet seen,

except some figures of satyrs and some tragic and comic masks. The simplicity is amazing. Nature is more complicated; a tree, for example, is a very complex thing. Art is an attempt to isolate certain objects and strip them of their natural accessories. It is a response to a desire, perhaps a selfish and immoral desire, to protect ourselves from reality. As we sat on the parapet of the Acropolis, beside those quiet, painless, even deathless works of art, the multitudinous din of the city rose and assailed our ears. It was a sound made up of many distinguishable elements, the tooting of automobile horns, the shriek of street-car wheels rounding a curve, the braying of asses, the crowing of cocks, the cries of newspaper vendors, the angry screams of women, the laughter of children, the mellow boom of church-bells. Vachel Lindsay might have made a poem out of it! but not even the poem would be simple. And this is life. It is perhaps a little more confused and futile in modern Athens than in any other city I have known. There is here, at all events, no selection, no aristocracy of noise. Somehow this roar, in contrast with the aloofness of the Acropolis, suggests the perfectly unethical and undemocratic attempt of our own country to restrict immigration. One hundred million people, in a land that can easily support five hundred millions, have the arrogance to say that it belongs to them,

simply because they hold prior possession, while
here are other millions without work who long to
begin life over again in the New World. In the abstract, whatever may be the expediency of our new
policy, it is quite immoral. The Greeks are more
generous, for they not only have admitted, but are
housing, clothing, and feeding a multitude of
strangers who as yet are absolutely dependent on
charity.

BARLOW'S DIARY. — Athens, March 7:

Keith is wallowing again in the slough of de-
spond between two ideals: on the one hand what he
terms the Christian Law of Equality and I call rank
Tolstoyism; on the other hand what we both agree
to name Individual Culture. He is capable of en-
joying the Parthenon, "this glorious work of fine
intelligence," as few men can; and I have caught
him unaware, when he was rapt in admiration. But
then the shadow crosses his face as he remembers
how few those are who have the good fortune to
stand where he stands and see what he sees. I am
pagan enough to desire more Individual Culture
than I am likely ever to obtain. A man cannot know
too much, whether of literature, history, or science;
he cannot be too appreciative of beauty. The problem comes up awkwardly sometimes in these Mediterranean cities, I must admit. When you have to

pass a dozen wretched fellow-creatures lying on the cold pavement, really crippled or blind, and holding out their hands for a small coin, you know you ought not to encourage begging, you know you couldn't possibly give enough to help them permanently, and yet you feel guilty if you don't do something. Individual culture is expensive. Not that I haven't known men and women who had so carefully employed their time as to become learned and refined with very small expenditure of money. I can understand Keith's being troubled with this problem of the relation between the bare economic life and the higher life of mankind; but to me it is perfectly plain that civilization alone, with its models of conduct, its impersonal and immaterial purposes, the select number of thoughts with which it peoples the mind, makes human existence worth while. He has more than once unburdened his soul to me on the subject of unrestricted immigration. I wish I could controvert all his arguments as easily as I handled his crazy ideas about the abstract right of people to move from country to country. If these Mediterranean cities are over-populated, it is not only our right but our duty to keep their unsuccessful individuals from swamping such civilization as we have either inherited or built up. Take our language, for example; nothing is more important for the future of the American people than that we should all speak and read one language and that it should be the same language that is used in England and other parts of the British Empire. Any profound variation, any extensive growth of dialects or of American peculiarities, would be sooner or later a cause of intellectual sterility. Copious immigration would put too great a strain upon our language, — the strain is already enormous — and upon our schools and teachers and writers. Keith was taken aback still farther when I pointed out that his view, or rather the effect of it upon the supply of cheap labor, would be cynically approved of by those " big capitalists " whom he detests. When it comes to the preservation of our speech and our literature and our spiritual union with the rest of that noble race to whom they belong as they do to us, I'm quite willing to let Keith say my attitude is aristocratic. Equality of opportunity as much as you please — equality of wealth even; but no levelling down of speech and thought!

KEITH'S DIARY. — Athens, March 8:

Barlow has been turning my principles inside out as usual, but though beaten in argument, I am unconvinced. Like many another weak logician, I had recourse to authority; yet, I fear, without affecting his opinions about the moral justification of art or of restricting immigration, two subjects that have got curiously mixed up together in our talks. I asked him to go with me to the Areopagus, or Mars' Hill, where St. Paul made to the Athenians that penetrating and engaging address of his. It is a barren rock, without a vestige of human occupation except a flight of steps cut in its flank, and rises within a bow-shot of the Acropolis, which in Paul's day was crowded with shining temples and no doubt thronged with worshippers of Athene. "Imagine the scene," I said to Barlow: " a travel-worn little Jew, surrounded by a small crowd of inquisitive Greeks who wanted to know why he had come to introduce a new religion into Athens, already so full of temples and statues of the gods. On the larger hill clustered the most celebrated and magnificent group of buildings in all Greece, gleaming milky-white against the deep blue sky, buildings dedicated to no barbaric or cruel cult, but to the worship of a deity who was conceived to be the patroness of refinement and humane arts. Can't you see him wave his arm towards the Parthenon — he *must* have made a sweeping gesture — when he said: ' God that made the world, and all things therein, seeing that he is Lord of heaven and earth, dwelleth not in temples made with hands ' ? What more would you have, Barlow? What is the value of all your churches and altars, in view of that declaration? Doesn't it condemn them all, in so far as they are supposed to possess any peculiar sanctity? Are not the Quakers and the other varieties of Puritans absolutely right? And by the way, with reference to our argument about immigration, look down the page here and see what that brave little man said: ' And hath made of one blood all nations of men for to dwell on the face of the earth.' " When I looked round to see what impression this had made, Barlow was halfway down the steps, hurrying back to the Acropolis; but in his place I almost felt another presence, firm as the rock we stood upon, unaltered in conviction, undaunted by the failure of the ages to accept his noble conception of God and man. " O unwearied traveller," I whispered, " go on, do not cease from your missionary journey through a world that is pagan still."

BARLOW'S DIARY. — Athens, March 9:

For once I have talked Keith down and made him admit I was right. Then for some reason he insisted on our taking a half hour of precious time, which was all needed for the Greek antiquities, and crawling up to the top of Mars' Hill, where he read me that speech of St. Paul from the Acts of the Apostles. It is a perfectly barren spot, and there are several better views of the Acropolis. I must say the speech was plucky and no end clever; indeed it was a generous, broad-minded, gentlemanly address.

Paul didn't run full tilt against all the Athenian customs and ideas, but acknowledged that they were good in the main. Of course he wound up by telling them that his religion was better than theirs, and so in most respects it was. Keith is right in one thing: Paul must have made a very opportune and significant gesture when he referred to "temples made with hands." I never before realized the power of that speech and the peculiarity of the situation in which it was delivered. Two ideals of life met there and challenged each other. Which has won? Well, it would be hard to say. Perhaps a third, less fine than either of them, has triumphed thus far. We are going to Rome in a week, where there are not a few temples made with hands.

KEITH'S DIARY. — Athens, March 10:

To-day we have visited the National Museum. It contains many famous statues and is, I suppose, the best place in the world for the study of Greek art. What impressed me above all were the carvings in relief, found in ancient cemeteries, and depicting domestic scenes at the moment when some member of the family is about to depart from this life. I purposely use the expression " depart from this life," for two of the suggestions generally connected with dying are absent, namely that of physical pain and dwindling and that of certitude in regard to a future state. Unless we misinterpreted the relation of the figures, the one who is standing and at whom the others appear to be looking represents in most cases the departing person. In the faces of all is a look of profound sorrow, unrelieved by hope: the parting, they understand, is forever. To take a typical example, a matron seated in a chair holds the hand of her son and gazes into his face; he stands before her speechless, while her lips appear to move. The father of the young man completes the group, waiting pensively for his turn to say farewell. On the countenance of the youth there is such a look of grief as a child might show when awed by the prospect of an impending trouble which it did not understand: a look of bewilderment, of dread, and of determination to be brave. Here we have the most authentic record of the ancient Greek view of death. There is no hint that though the body perish the soul continues to exist. The young man in my example appears to be in perfect health. No mark of decay is on him nor, as I remember, on any of the figures of the departing. Scorn of the flesh, contempt for life, a sense of the inferiority of the body to the soul, or indeed any distinction between body and soul, are not indicated. A characteristically Christian account of the last earthly parting would show the triumph of spirit and the humiliation of flesh. And the effect desired would be to confirm the beholder's faith in a future personal existence. It troubles me to think that the truth, in a matter of such universal and infinite importance should have been withheld from a people so highly developed as the ancient Greeks; unless indeed —

BARLOW'S DIARY. — Athens, March 10:

I have never felt so deeply the eternizing power of art as I did to-day in the National Museum. The steles, or funeral reliefs, for instance, simply annihilate twenty-four hundred years and bring you into the households of people who lived before Pericles or Plato. Ancient war differed much from modern war; ancient worship was unlike modern worship; we need a good deal of help from the antiquarians when we study the carvings on the Acropolis which depict fighting and religious ceremonies. But death and grief were just the same then as now. As Keith was quick to see, however, pagan art represented them quite differently from Christian art. The body and its life or soul went out together, like the wax and the flame of a taper, and they went out completely, with no prospect of being rekindled as one may sometimes relight a candle by touching a burning match to the smoke before it cools. It is strange that while Christian funeral sculpture usually represents the survivors as disconsolate and the departing person as very confident, the ancient Greek steles show the reverse. In them the departing one looks puzzled, though resolute and almost resigned, while the faces and attitudes of the surviving relatives speak encouragement. There is no weeping on either part, no rending of garments, no abandonment to despair. The emotions that must inevitably have been felt, — disappointment, grief, and hopelessness — are suppressed, and that too without apparent constraint. The decorum of these scenes must have been habitual and inbred, not forced. The harmony and order of family life are preserved even in these supremely agonizing moments: parents retain their places of honor; children retain their bearing of affectionate respect. That which raises my opinion of the candor of the Greeks to the highest pitch is the fact that death is represented in these tablets exactly as it must, I am sure, appear to the mind of anyone who is in an unaffected condition: I mean free from theory on the subject. I am not for a moment wishing to suggest that one at least of the opinions about a future life with which mankind has been either tormented or consoled may not be true; what I like in those Greek sculptors is that they made faithful pictures of a state of society in which the acceptance of death was very simple and natural. We ought, I think, to be always ready and glad to discover any

universal or widespread good in humanity, any
virtue common to all ages and to all peoples. It is
only a narrow and crabbed kind of religious feeling which would blind men to the nobility of such
a way of facing death as the Greek monuments reveal. It was not ecstatic, and therefore not liable to
grotesque error. The serene grace that almost sub-
dues the poignancy of everlasting separation in
these domestic scenes is all the more admirable because it is the result not of faith but of experience;
for upon experience rather than metaphysics or
tradition or sporadic revelation must a really universal view of life and human destiny be founded.
What I mean by culture, when Keith and I are talking seriously, is a wide and sympathetic knowledge
of experience.

VINO DI ORVIETO

There come perfect hours in a lifetime, and it were "a sullenness against nature" to make no record of them. Towards the end of April, called by the sweet season of the year from the bewildering noise, the dirt, and the danger of Roman streets, and weary of that heaviness with which Rome sooner or later burdens the mind, we wandered forth to seek change and refreshment of spirit. Free as birds on the wing, we passed several towns that seemed to beckon to us from airy heights above the valley of the Tiber, and came to rest only when we had reached the foot of the great rock on which stands Orvieto. It was there we spent our perfect hours.

Staring from the railroad platform up to the mountain-top, it seemed unlikely that we should ever arrive without wings, but a little car of the funicular or switchback variety solved the problem, and in a few minutes we were a thousand feet above the plain. The town wall lay yet some distance beyond, and to this fact we were to owe a pleasant acquaintance with a fellow-traveller; for when the omnibus that met the car had been filled to over-

flowing with ladies and a young fellow of a breed
not noted for good manners, I found myself left behind with an elderly Englishman, who, like myself,
had not cared to scramble for a seat. I knew by the
look of him that he would not, and also that we
should enjoy a walk and talk together. One meets in
travelling agreeable people of almost every nation,
but in my experience none more attractive than the
English. They are seldom in a hurry, or selfishly
pushing and elbowing, or too offish and suspicious
to engage in conversation. And they are by far the
best informed travellers to be encountered any-
where — not so full perhaps of guide-book directions as the Germans, but much richer in personal
experience. The English are at home in the world,
and bring with them, wherever they go, the quiet,
self-respecting, yet friendly, manners of their own
country. The French, if they ventured in any considerable numbers beyond their own frontiers,
would, no doubt, add much to the social pleasures
of travel; but they stay at home. The result of our
" Anglo-Saxon calm " was that both our parties
had the good fortune to be turned away from the
principal hotel and were therefore obliged to go to
the Albergo della Posta. This quaint hostelry is
situated in a back street so narrow that persons
walking in it could hardly escape being crushed
against the walls if a large vehicle were to go

through it at the same time. But once inside the inn, there is space enough and to spare. The entrance hall is a large vaulted room, with a door opening on the right into a clean little restaurant, a passage at the back leading past an enormous kitchen, lined with brass pots and pans, to a bright garden, and on the left a stone staircase winding away to the mysteries of the upper floors. Of good augury was the fact that the proprietor and his servants were content to address us in their own beautiful language and did not inflict upon us that painfully acquired and seldom copious English or French, or that absurd mixture of English, French, and German, which hampers the speaker and robs the guest of his own perhaps equally bad Italian.

We decided to inspect our quarters briefly and then go at once to the cathedral while the afternoon light was at its best; but the house proved to be so picturesque that we were fain to linger in it. The back windows looked upon an irregular court, in the sunny depths of which lay the garden we had seen from the entrance hall. Little effort had been made to beautify the court; yet it was very pretty and romantic. The glittering whitewashed walls of the inn, with arched galleries, ran along two sides of it, and on the remaining sides were the irregular gables of other buildings, with flowers growing in pots on the window-sills and wild plants blooming

where they had struck root on the cornices and
among the tiles, and cats asleep on ledges, and an
old woman hanging out clothes to dry on a flat
roof, and a tinkling fountain casting jets of water
into a pool where goldfish floated in absurdly ma-
jestic circles, and at the back of all a grand tower
of dark stone with an immense clock-face near its
top. Rooks or crows, or some other birds of the
black-coated, cawing kind, were dodging in and out
of holes in this mediæval structure and flashing in
the sunlight. It had no other openings in the side
that was visible from where we stood, and, with its
hundred feet of vertical wall, was the more impressive for being so monotonously plain. In spite of its
evident antiquity the lines of its courses and the
edges of its corners were perfectly sharp. We felt
that it had been built for defense and not originally
for the peaceful purpose of holding a big clock.
Along the galleries we could see into the cell-like
bedrooms, which were flooded with light like certain interiors by Hoogh and Gerard Dou. Our own
room, too, was truly conventual, with walls three
feet thick and a simplicity and severity of aspect
that were quite remote from the ornate mouldings
and frescoes of many Italian hotels. We made up
our minds that the Albergo della Posta had once
been a monastery and the courtyard a cloister.

The bell in the tower striking five mellow notes

as we stood at our window, we turned away, not
without reluctance, to visit the cathedral. We found
the streets paved evenly from wall to wall with
broad smooth flagstones, and quite clean. There
were few people astir, and we saw no motor-cars,
and indeed scarcely a vehicle of any kind. After
Rome, in whose narrow, twisting streets the danger
of being run over is very great and the uncertainty
about which way foot-passengers will turn is a constant annoyance, this was Arcadian peace. There
appears to be no rule of the road for people afoot
in Italy. It was so in Dante's time, for he mentions
as a rare bit of ingenuity the fact that during the
papal jubilee of 1300 such a rule was enforced
temporarily on the bridge of St. Angelo because of
the great throng. He declares also that it was a per-
manent arrangement in one of the circles of Hell;
from which we may infer that the Italian mind
abhors this first principle of municipal order.

Walking thus, free to use my eyes for pleasure
rather than safety, I presently beheld a glory in the
air before us. Above the dark mass of clustering
houses rose a triangle of shining gold, held in position, as it were, by the firm azure of the sky. Turning to watch the effect on my companion, I saw her
face catch the glow and reflect it in a smile of glad-
some wonder. After the ugliness of nearly all the
churches in Rome — ugliness, heaviness and in-

congruous setting — the first glimpse of this brilliant architectural jewel gave us a sense of joy and
freedom. It was in sooth a glorious vision that burst
upon us when we turned into the square before the
west front. The cathedral stands in a clear, open
space, untouched by any other building. The eye, as
it passes round its flanks to left and to right, leaps
away to mountains many miles distant or to the
vault of heaven. The walls of the structure were laid
in alternate courses of black basalt and white lime-
stone. It speaks much for the general harmony of
the work and the splendor of the Italian atmosphere
that this audacious feat has succeeded, and no
doubt time has softened what must at first have been
a too violent contrast, by turning the white to yellow and covering the black with a patine of green-
ish gray dust. Nevertheless, some observers find it
too sharp for their taste, although it is here more
toned down than in the sister cathedral of Siena.
The world of art can well afford to keep gratefully
two such bright jewels, even though, or just because,
they produce an effect totally different from the
religious awe that emanates from York Minster or
the miracle of Chartres. They are, among the
"many mansions," a peculiar and precious pair.

Except for this gayety of color-design, the side-
walls are exceedingly plain. There are no disen-
gaged or flying buttresses, and over many square

yards of surface there are few windows and these not large. Nothing is more destructive of architectural impressiveness than a superfluity of openings, and the small proportion of them here lends an air of grave dignity to this church, which in some respects is surpassingly gorgeous. The façade, notably, is the very reverse of those old Gothic fronts that awe the beholder in northern countries. There is no mystery about it, no suggestiveness of anything beyond the power of human expression. The artists who planned and executed it were sure of themselves and of their theology, accomplished in the ways of this world, and perfectly confident about that other world which it was their business to make clear to men's eyes. The design is simple, the details are distinct, the colors as rich as possible. On the lower part, where they can be easily seen, are innumerable sculptured figures, representing Biblical stories and ecclesiastical legends, in particular the separation of good and bad people on the day of judgment. It was reassuring to observe that the good outnumbered the bad in the proportion of about ten to one, an unusual liberality for a mediæval work.

No further relaxation of theological fury is shown, however, in the character of the picture. The damned are being clawed and bitten by demons, in a scene which reminds one of a horrible episode in the "Inferno" of Dante, who was a contemporary of the pupils of Niccolo Pisano, who carved these vivid reliefs. The portals are formed in part of slender columns studded with glittering mosaic, the small green and red stones being individually visible a hundred yards away, so bright they are. Narrow, flat, vertical surfaces, equally adorned with mosaics in most ingenious geometrical patterns, lead the eye upward to the three pediments, one representing the nave and the others the side aisles. Here is the most burning splendor, for here are three superbly brilliant triangular spaces blazing with blue and gold and crimson, in which are depicted the Baptism of Christ, the Annunciation, and in the central and highest picture the Coronation of the Madonna. In these lively paintings is no dim uncertainty, no groping after the unknown, no feeling even that the figures and the stories are symbolical; all is firm conviction, both in regard to the dogmas and to the legends with which they were associated; indeed, the dogmas themselves and whatever moral instruction they may be supposed to convey are lost sight of in the concrete presentment of "fact."

We sank in perfect content upon the stone bench that runs along the houses on the opposite side of the square, studying this wonder till the westering sun had ceased to illumine the lower parts. Then through the central doorway, which was wide open, we entered the nave. After the gaudy and crushing chaos of bronze and gilt at St. Peter's and many other Roman churches, it was a great pleasure to find the interior severely plain. It was airy, too, and luminous. Swallows were darting along the ceiling as if in token of this naturalness. The walls of the choir and transepts are covered with frescoes by Fra Angelico and Signorelli, but we reserved them for morning light and returned to the warmer air outside. The grassy close (an unusual feature in Italy) on the north side of the cathedral is bounded by a row of plain dwellings coated with gray plaster, in which the age-long growth of minute lichens has produced a rusty brown agreeable to the eye and harmonizing well with green shutters, the only wooden objects in sight. Several infants were toddling about in the grass that grew irregularly over the acre or two of ground, and swallows, perhaps younger but much more agile, were swooping and twittering not far above their heads. Two schoolboys, who were even lovelier than the cathedral or the blue sky, approached us with modest looks and hesitating steps and asked if we had any foreign postage-stamps to spare. They were making collections, they said; and we were to find in the course of our sojourn that all the boys of Orvieto were smitten with the same craze. When our little friends heard we were Americans, their eyes glistened: they needed American stamps very particularly, for Uruguay and Bolivia were still lacking in their collections. It was hard for them to grasp the statement that, though Americans, we were not from Uruguay nor Bolivia. At their polite request, we took their names and addresses, and they shall hear from us when we have rare stamps. I also cut off some Greek stamps from my passport for them. When they saw the photograph which disfigures it, the boys held their breath and whispered " Mussolini "; from which several inferences may be drawn, the ever-present expectation of seeing the dictator's picture, for one, and also that he is no beauty. The Orvietans themselves are handsome, as a rule, with fine regular features and a high color. Bidding farewell to the boys proved superfluous, for we met them again and again, until the acquaintance ripened into that quick friendship which is possible between grown people and children. They told us about their school and their lessons, and showed us their books, and talked about the nations of the earth and the stamps thereof.

An Italian town preserves a distinct rhythm. If you go out early in the morning — and nine o'clock is early — you find the shops not yet open, and the street-corners occupied by bronzed, solid-looking farmers, trading, no doubt. Then from about ten

till one the ordinary shopping of the day is trans-
acted. For the next three hours the streets are
empty; stores and offices are closed; people are eating and taking their siesta. From four to six the
place swarms with children, and from six to nine
the ladies and men of leisure and all others, in fact,
who are not kept in by some overpowering necessity, come forth and stroll. This rhythm was exactly
preserved at Orvieto during our stay.

Whether we went through the streets in the early
hours or the late, when peasants were selling vege-
tables, fruit, and flowers, or when the fashionable
townsfolk were engaged in public sociability, we
were struck with the distinctness and similarity of
facial type. It appeared frequently in perfection
among children of both sexes and among women.
Its characteristics were sweetness of expression, a
refinement of feature that seemed to speak of intellectual capacity, and the rich tints that betoken
health. These Umbrians are perhaps more vigorous
and robust than the Tuscan mountaineers who come
into Siena on a feast day. Blue eyes and fair hair
are less common here than in the regions about
Pistoia. The soft black eyes of the Orvietans glow
with a splendor reflected from ruddier cheeks,
burnt by a slightly warmer sun and fanned perchance by a steadier wind. The Italian peasants, as
a class, are, I think, the finest-looking human beings

in the world, not merely as objects pleasing to the eye, but because their faces and figures betoken grace, frankness, intelligence, and goodwill. This is more than I can say for the so-called middle class or *bourgeoisie*, who constitute the bulk of the urban population, or for the less easily defined and far less numerous upper class. The best one can say for Orvieto is that her people nearly all look like peasants. This is high praise. A book, rich with illustrations, might be written, and should be written, on the Peasantry of Europe. Its author would, I believe, find it possible to maintain that the peasants in general surpass the rest of the population in health, beauty, manners, morality, industry and happiness, and eminent among them all would stand those of Italy.

I have mentioned the almost total absence of motor nuisances in this mountain town. The great god Gasoline is not worshipped there, and men lead safe and quiet lives. In one or two other ways also we were reminded of the Golden Age, before the world, and especially America, became standardized. The old handicrafts are still practised in Orvieto. The saddler in his little shop plies the awl and waxed cord on horse-collars and breechings; the shoemaker, not yet a mere cobbler, sticks to his last; the tailor can be seen through his open door sitting cross-legged on the table; coopers, amid shavings and barrel-staves, wield the draw-knife; cabinet-makers plane and fit and polish bureaus and desks and elegant little boxes; we saw in the cavernous depths of a vast basement an old woman at the loom; we stumbled upon two men and a boy twisting long lines in a ropewalk; and what made us most homesick for the vanished life of our childhood was a little shop where two men were building a carriage. Is there any small town left in America, I wonder, where all these pleasant old trades are still pursued as household industries?

Our last evening in Orvieto was spent in circumambulating the walls. Not trusting entirely in the vertical cliffs within whose unbroken circuit the pre-Roman Etruscan tribe once clustered, the Romans, who called the town Urbs Vetus, and their mediæval successors, crowned the edge of these precipices with a wall of stupendous masonry. We found ourselves at sunset in a particularly secluded angle of the wall. It was an irregular area, hemmed in on the west by a parapet over which we looked into an appalling abyss, and shut off on the south by two black ancient houses and on the east by a neglected church. A woman sat spinning with a distaff at the door of one of the houses, and three of her neighbors stood beside her in loud debate. We gazed out over the vast gulf of air to the mountains that rimmed the horizon, noting the white farmhouses scattered like dice over the dim plain below, and here and there a monastery, with its belfry and cemetery and group of cypresses. A tremulous purple flood seemed rising from the depths, as if presently to fill the valley and brim over into the world of light outside. The little church behind us was not glorified by the sunset blaze, but only made to look disconsolate in its forlorn and squalid setting. Some touch of faded nobility in its face invited us to enter. A shabby interior it seemed at first, but, as our eyes grew accustomed to the gloom, we perceived many signs of ancient and outworn beauty. Through the whitewash that covered the walls and columns old frescoes faintly smiled; old faces vivid still, and doubtless preserving the features of originals who lived ages ago in Orvieto, were struggling once more against oblivion in those few moments when the beams of the setting sun came level through the door which we held open. We turned away slightly depressed.

We were not depressed, but much exalted, upon leaving Orvieto the next day, for we felt that we had been happy there, and were old enough to know the value of such a vintage and the folly of draining the cup of the dregs. It was mid-afternoon when we climbed into a cross-country autobus, in the Piazza, having decided to go over the mountains to Perugia by this means rather than by railway. A young Danish painter whom we had met at the inn chanced to be sauntering past with his easel and canvas on his back, and stopped to say, in slow pleasant tones: " Fare-you-well! " And then came a delightful surprise: it was two hours before we lost sight of Orvieto. We sank into the valley of the Tiber, and thought we had seen the last of those cliffs and towers; but anon we were climbing the eastern wall of the valley, and — " Look," we said, " there is Orvieto still! " The three sharp triangles of the roof of the cathedral were unmistakable, and so was our clock-tower, where we knew the rooks were talking. Half an hour later, from a yet loftier point, a turn of the road brought the little city in sight again, and, although miles away, we recognized it plainly. Once more, and twenty times more, as we climbed towards the line where the snows of March had but recently melted, we saw our friendly town, and " Fare-you-well! " it seemed to cry. At last, just before we crossed the divide and began to rush down into San Vengano, we caught one more glimpse: " There it is! There it is still! Fare-you-well, Orvieto! "

TWO OLD FOGIES IN HOLLAND

Extremes are enticing. This fact explains polar expeditions. It also accounts for our desire to go to the Helder, the most northern point in the province of North Holland, where the waters of the Zuider Zee clash twice a day with those of the North Sea. Here, we were told in Amsterdam, was a very tall lighthouse which twinkles to another on the island of Texel, and so on, by way of Flieland and Ter Schelling, to Denmark and Norway, thus binding in a fellowship of helpfulness the outer fringe of those lands from which our English race rose into being and when it drew its tenacity, its love of the hard-won soil, and its daring on the deep. We thought we would rather behold the flash of that light than the glare of all the cafés in Amsterdam and rather hear the rush of those waves than the blare of motor-horns. There is also a great sea-wall at the Helder, miles and miles of marvellous masonry, which protects the vast garden that the Dutch have made out of sand and swamps and filled with one of the most industrious and illustrious populations in the world. We had spent many hours of thrilling joy in the picture galleries of Rotterdam,

The Hague, Haarlem, and Amsterdam, and then on stepping out into the streets and wandering through one or two villages had discovered that the models of the paintings we had so much admired were still living in their descendants. Since Nature, as Dante says, is the parent of Art and the daughter of God, we felt that it would be almost impious to neglect the mother for the child. And obviously the place from which to make her acquaintance in Holland is not a car window but the deck of a boat.

Thus it came to pass that on a sunshiny morning in early July we stepped aboard the Alkmaar packet, at her moorings in the harbor of Amsterdam, not much caring what her destination might be nor when she reached it, nor even when she started, for the interest of the voyage began long before her screw made its first revolution. It pleased us to remark that the pedestrians in the streets, being rational, practical, and withal social people, were more strict in observing the law of the road than the less disciplined inhabitants of South European cities, where everybody bumps along as he pleases. The Dutch keep not only to the right side of the pavement, but to the right-hand pavement. We also noticed gratefully and put down as another little mark of high civilization, the fact that people did not stare at us, though no doubt there was something outlandish in our appearance. The Dutch have had a long and varied experience of the world; their empire is far-flung; they govern about seven times their own number of East and West Indians; their shipping and their geographical position make them neighbors to all the earth. Consequently they have a worldly-wise tolerance of what is foreign.

While we were commenting on these acquirements of reason and experience, the little steamboat had backed almost imperceptibly into the maze of river traffic and was now passing an interminable double row of warehouses, many of them bearing names of foreign ports, among which I noted Rangoon, Marseilles, Assam, Singapore, Baltimore, and Wilmington. Soon we were floating high above green pastures, where black and white cattle of the breed we call Holstein were frisking after their morning feed. Gardens of country-houses, with bowers at the water's edge where families take coffee and smoke and talk, and " roses, roses all the way," lined the canal for a few miles; and then began the more truly rural spectacle, farmhouses close to the dykes that held up the water of our highway, and level meadows stretching back to the next intersecting canal or dyke. At short intervals we came to villages and towns, catching glimpses down their streets, which generally consisted of canals with narrow brick sidewalks, shaded by rows of young elms.

Human life in field and farmhouse and village was going on almost precisely as one sees it in the paintings of Vermeer and Terborg and Hoogh. Our voyage was like a trip through an endless gallery of the old Dutch masters. It was as if all their landscapes and street scenes treasured in a hundred museums throughout the world had come back for an old home gathering. Here a group of cattle belonged plainly to the breed of Cuyp; there a glimpse into a village street showed us the very men and women of Ostade; and again a girl's face at an open window said, "I am by Gerard Dou." When the canal widened into a lake, as it sometimes did, the ruffled water and the sail-boats leaning to the breeze were autographed "van der Meer." All was as quiet as a picture-gallery too, for no sounds were audible save the swish of ripples against the reeds and the twitter of skylarks in the blue. And we, the spectators, were as detached from the green world through which we moved as a visitor in a gallery is from the pictures on the wall, no one turning his head to look at us or waving a hand to greet us. The most startling reminder of an old master was one elderly woman whom we passed so close that we could see the color of her shrewd little eyes, the thousand criss-cross wrinkles in her cheeks and forehead and chin, and the texture of the bodice that restrained her amplitude. We knew

at least three famous portaits by Frans Hals for
which she might have been the model. At the next
stop the mail bag was picked up and carried off by
quite a modern-looking girl, more beautiful than
any that the old masters ever succeeded in painting,
and reminding me of a young lady I saw performing the same office at a lonely landing on the James
river, twenty-one years ago.

Hour after hour passed thus in sweet content,
until to our regret we reached Alkmaar, beyond
which the packet does not go. Here we had a long
wait, through and beyond the sleepy noon hour, in
a little café, where we procured some refreshment
and also some entertainment. The place was kept
by a wise-looking but far from handsome man, and
his fat little boy, and a dog named Mux. The three
men and one old woman who came in as fellow cus-
tomers had enough individuality and plainness of
feature to give them a place in one of Jan Steen's
tavern scenes, and the sanded wooden floor would
have been in keeping too. Our solicitude about
catching a boat for the north was deprecated by our
host, who stood on a chair to look along the canal,
while the fat boy lay down to get a better view in
our interest, and Mux went out to see for himself.
Our host showed us the dog's photograph while he
was gone, thus avoiding any inflammation of canine
vanity.

Do not blame me, impatient reader, accustomed to automats and automobiles, for dwelling at so much length upon a noon hour spent in a Dutch coffee-house. Hours of peaceful happiness are none too frequent in this world, and I should like you to catch some reflection of the sunlight which lay upon the yellow floor of that room, and could wish you to hear, as we still hear in memory, the gentle tones of those kindly, simple folk. We understood few of their words, yet the meaning was clear enough. To anyone who knows English and German, Dutch sounds tantalizingly familiar. The language of the heart being the same everywhere, goodwill, intelligence, and courtesy, which were lavished upon us in Holland, made the difference of language seem unimportant. Moreover, we could read Dutch if we could not speak it. At last the smaller boat that plies between Alkmaar and the Helder poked her nose round a corner and tied up in front of the house; and with friendly farewells from man and boy and dog we stepped on board.

The scenery now was more monotonous and even more rural than that of the forenoon. Vast meadows intersected by narrow canals stretched away on both sides, dotted with cattle and at large intervals with farmhouses, of which the high-peaked garrets serve for storing hay. Every house had its windbreak of fruit-trees and its gay flower-garden, and

here and there a windmill made solemn gestures.
The level of our canal was higher than the fields,
and the whole district was protected from the sea to
westward by a line of dunes. This is really more
than a line; it is a tract, in some parts several miles
wide, of sand-hills driven up from the beach by the
west wind and tossed into the semblance of a mountain range. The sand would be blown inland and
wasted, besides ruining the pastures, were it not
held down by heather and gorse and other persist-
ent plants, which say, " No, you must stop here! "
The dunes present an aspect of singular wildness
when viewed from one of their tumultuous peaks.
One might easily be lost and wander helpless for
hours in their winding hollows. An imaginative
Dutch child, who had only read of mountains,
might see in the dunes his Apennines or Andes, so
sharp is the contrast between them and the flat pastures or the level ocean.

Late in the long midsummer evening we arrived
at the Helder. It is the principal station of the
Dutch navy, and as we walked to our hotel we
passed a handsome marine hospital, the vice-ad-
miral's headquarters, and several warships moored
beside the quay. At first I was rather pleased to find
that a kermess or fair was in full blast in the street
below the windows of our hotel, having happy
memories of one I had witnessed more than forty

years ago. From the mysterious inner parts of a merry-go-round were soaring forth the strains of an old tune, which I had not heard since then, making alive once more the romance of peasant life, folk-song, and waltzing, and golden youth of bygone days. To be perfectly frank, we grew rather tired of that melody in the next five afternoons and nights, and it seemed as if all the boys and girls of North Holland would be rendered permanently dizzy by riding those wooden horses. Round and round they went, to the strains of that broad, slow, golden music, round and round, and up and down, screaming with delight.

The pleasant little town, with its dark canals, and avenues of lime-trees, and well scrubbed housefronts, and shining windowpanes, nestles close behind the dune, which is strengthened on its northern flank by massive layers of Norwegian granite. Along the top runs a broad brick pavement. Outside, the waves of the North Sea beat in vain, and over the clinging grasses that master the sand the winds whistle hurtlessly. This great rampart, five or six miles long, lies like a bent arm enfolding town and fortress and the wide expanse of North Holland.

In the five days we spent behind that sheltering arm or strolling upon it from shoulder to fingertips, we saw no foreigners, except half a dozen

English yachtsmen who tied up their pretty craft one evening alongside the quay. The hotel was excellent and wholly Dutch, not in the least international or standardized. We found time to read the newspapers, and it is to be remarked that these are not merely newspapers but daily magazines; for besides a quite abundant supply of telegrams from all parts of the world, they contain well written articles on subjects of literary, scientific, economic, religious, and historical interest. One can get all that is worth while out of a French daily in five minutes; ten are usually enough for most American dailies; but a first-class Dutch paper provides good reading for an hour. In one of the Amsterdam papers which I saw at the Helder there was, for example, a series of three or four extremely able letters from Grand Rapids, Michigan, describing the life of the Dutch who constitute one-third of the population of that Western city.

Very noticeable in Holland is the absence of a rowdy element. There is not, so far as we could perceive, that objectionable creature whom a friend of ours calls "the village tough," the fellow who goes about with a chip on his shoulder and is to be found in every American town, with scowling face, lazy habits, and filthy language, a product of the old-time saloon, — "the corner boy" he is called in Ireland, I believe. No doubt the great seaports,

Rotterdam and Amsterdam, could show something similar; but it is hardly fair to include great seaports when one is looking for the essential character of a country. The human background in Europe is the peasantry, for the most part unspoiled, healthy, industrious, and of steady morals. Economically it is the basis of society, producing the food and the raw material for most of the clothing. In every country it is the main support of the church. It supplies fresh family stocks for what is called the middle class. If it resists innovations both good and bad, it holds out against extravagance and vice. In some parts of Europe, especially Italy, the peasantry are so superior in physique and in morality to the townspeople, taken as a whole, that the latter seem to belong to a different race. Between the Italian peasant and most of that superincumbent mass who buy and resell and consume the produce of his toil and weave his political destiny for him, regardless of his advantage, the balance is altogether in favor of the healthy, handsome, happy tiller of the soil. We received the impression, however, that in Holland the town-dwellers were not inferior to the farming people and that the population as a whole had attained a higher level of civilization than in any other country with which we were at all well acquainted, outside of Great Britain.

The traditional notions about foreign parts which we inherit from older generations or have picked up from superficially written books of travel are often curiously inexact. The Dutch, for example, are not particularly slow and phlegmatic. I have found them quicker in business than the Germans and the French. Nor has the flatness of their land rendered them commonplace in spirit or unimaginative. They have through the centuries been distinguished for their love of flowers, of brilliant costumes, and of landscape, and for their ability to copy the forms and colors of nature. I have long been of the opinion that Mark Twain, in his "Tramp Abroad" and other books of travel, rendered a distinct disservice to us Americans, lowering our respect for much that is dignified and noble, feeding our national vanity, and encouraging our silly tendency to scoff at whatever we see in foreign lands that differs from what we have been accustomed to at home. I daresay those who have caught the trick from Mark Twain would have been irritated or foolishly amused by the old quiet ways of the Helder and of North Holland in general, but to us, who never liked his irreverent smartness, these people seemed to have won by heroic fortitude most of the things in life that are worth while, and we contemplated with profound respect the scene of their struggles and success.

The sea bathing at the Helder is of the best, and we had our share of it, finding the water of the North Sea warmer than the name sounds. The sun appeared afraid of it, however, for he took his dip reluctantly, sidling into the waves at about half past nine.

We tried in vain to get a skipper to take us across the Zuider Zee in a sailboat, to Harlingen on the coast of Friesland, and were obliged to go less adventurously, though scarcely less romantically, by steamer from Enkhuizen to Stavoren. Our objective was Leeuwarden, in the heart of the province, a town remarkable, even in the Netherlands, for its calm decorum, its clean and well shaded streets, and its general air of prosperity; and it is also celebrated for two peculiar features, a massive brick tower in the Gothic style, from the top of which one beholds the wide expanse of that most northern part of the kingdom, and a museum of Frisian art and antiquities, which is a nearly perfect thing of its kind. The collections in this museum are almost strictly local. Among them are half a dozen rooms that have been transported *in toto* from the village of Hindeloopen, complete in every respect, walls, ceilings, furniture, and utensils, and looking as if their occupants had just stepped out. I had quite recently visited at Pennsburg, in Pennsylvania, a museum of Pennsylvania-

German antiquities which has a similar scope. On a vastly larger scale there is the London Museum. In Florence there is the Palazzo Davanzati. Martha Washington's old home at Fredericksburg, Virginia, is an example on a smaller scale and with a more restricted purpose, and so is Washington's Headquarters at Rocky Hill, New Jersey. Mount Vernon is a splendid example of this more specialized kind. Every locality with a peculiar and romantic history, such as the Cumberland Valley in Pennsylvania, should have its historical museum, even though few could draw upon a field so rich in human antiquity as Friesland.

But Leeuwarden was our turning-point, and we had to come back to a less serene world. The pale gold of northern sunlight, gleaming along the lakes and canals, the scarcely audible swish of water-grasses lifted by the swell from the passing boat, the quiet voices of the people, left for memory a sense of peace and satisfaction rare indeed, and we were thankful to have spent even one week in North Holland and Friesland.

IF DANTE WERE ALIVE

The year of Dante's death, 1321, was at the climax of the Middle Ages. As far as Christendom extended, the note of that era, notwithstanding many harsh discords, was unity. In Western Europe, certainly, there were, broadly speaking, one theology, one visible Church, two or at most three general types of civil government, one system of instruction, one dominant philosophy, and throughout most of that territory one type of land-tenure and military obligation. The memory of Roman unity had not faded, and the hope of attaining it once more was bright. Dante is in no other respect so representative of the mediæval mind as in his desire for unity. Towards unity flowed the four main currents of his life.

His political effort may, at a superficial glance, appear to have been made in the direction of a division and not in the interest of unity. He was the author of a treatise, "De Monarchia," in which he argued for a differentiation between the functions of Church and State, — the Pope to mind things spiritual, and the Emperor to rule in secular affairs. But observe that they were to govern the world jointly, in a union of purpose, though according to the maxim which Dante himself utters: "Quod potest fieri per unum, melius est per unum fieri quam per plura." If the head of the Holy Roman Empire had really established his authority over the whole of Western Europe, including all the petty principalities and city republics of Italy and the clans and kingdoms of the British Isles, with the Pope at his side as the spiritual representative of Christ, there would have been a better chance for unity than with either of these potentates usurping the functions of the other. Dante's political ideal was not realized, but his "De Monarchia" probably had some effect in checking such usurpations and leading to the modern theory that the separation of Church and State is more conducive to concord than a specious and irritating union can ever be.

Dante's effort in the field of philosophy was to demonstrate the unity of revelation with natural and historical truth; in other words, to coördinate Christian theology and the teachings of Aristotle. He made attempts not only in the sphere of metaphysics and ethics, but even in biology and astronomy, to show that the Bible and Aristotle, used conjointly, could explain all mysteries and furnish an organon or instrument for further research. Aristotle, we must remember, was for Dante, as for mediæval thinkers in general, the supreme authority in science as well as the fountain-head of speculation. Now, however vain it may seem to a modern man to suppose either that Aristotle was an adequate authority in science or that all of the vast number of remarks made in the Bible upon an infinity of subjects can be reconciled with Aristotle's teachings, we must remember that for a period varying from two hundred to four hundred years, according to locality, this union of authorities was supposed to have been established, and that for good or ill it ruled the scholastic world.

Dante's effort in the field of philology was likewise made in the interest of unity. It is safe to say that no other man we have ever heard of, not even Martin Luther, accomplished so much as Dante towards establishing, indeed almost creating, a language. The Greeks, had he done such a work among them, would have given him divine honors, with Orpheus and those other few, who, in Sidney's phrase, were " the first of that country that made pens deliverers of their knowledge to their posterity." In his " De Vulgari Eloquio," Dante tells us of his purpose and recounts, in part, the process by which he selected the dialect of Tuscany and elevated it above all other Italian dialects — Bolognese, Roman, Venetian, Apulian, and the rest — as the literary idiom of the peninsula. If ever a man performed a godlike task, it was this; for consider how slowly and by the operation of how many and varied causes dialects generally rise to such eminence. Dante thus gave to all Italians who have lived since his time a common literary language. In so doing he opened to the Italian people a hope of intellectual unity and placed in their possession the chief instrument for accomplishing that hope.

The fourth of Dante's great efforts was literary, and here again his purpose was to establish unity. He attempted to write, and he succeeded in writing, a universal poem, — a poem packed with all the learning of his time, glowing with all the color of his country's beauty and charm, vibrant with the strain of contemporary politics, tumultuous with private passion and family feud, arduous in its pursuit of philosophic truth, vast in design, minute in detail, and all subdued and harmonized to one clear chord, — the unity of the faith and of the knowledge of the Son of God. It is the chief single source of information about mediæval man. It is still true to Italian character. It is the supreme Christian poem. It is, I believe, the greatest individual work of art created by any one human being. I have no desire to claim for the "Divine Comedy" freshness and breadth equal to the freshness and breadth of the "Iliad" or the "Odyssey"; or moral truth and motive power equal to the moral truth and motive power of the Bible; or vigor, splendor, and variety equal to the vigor, splendor, and variety of Shakespeare's plays; although these qualities it indeed possesses in magnificent profusion. The " Divine Comedy " is remarkable, even among these master-works, for the strict unity which binds into a perfect effect all the attributes, each in good measure, which make Homer and the Bible and Shakespeare glorious. It is the universal poem.

It is unfortunately true that there were many elements of discord at work in the world at the opening of the fourteenth century, and that Dante himself was envenomed with partisan hate and blinded by personal prejudice. These evils were nowhere so devastating as in Italy, and Dante was not only an Italian of the Italians, but a man of genius, and for that reason a man of intense intellectual passion. But his ideal, which he knew to be greater than his genius and purer than his passions, was the ideal of unity, and with all his disappointments, his countenance, when he died, six hundred years ago, may well have been irradiated with the glad knowledge that to a marvellous degree his dream had come true. Though from a modern point of view he may seem to have been arguing for a closer coöperation between Church and State than would be tolerated today, yet as compared with other mediæval jurists and philosophers he was an advocate of separation; and no doubt a sense of this fact, kept alive by later poets, helped mightily to bring to pass, in due season the political unification of Italy and to restrict the Roman Church to spiritual dominion. Though it is true that the scholastic philosophy has been reduced to dust by "the unimaginable touch of time," nevertheless he deserves eternal gratitude for illustrating it so brilliantly and withal so naïvely. The Italian language, which he chose from among a dozen local dialects and dignified with his poetry, is a living and perpetual testimony to his foresight. His great poem endures, and seems likely to survive the ruins of all the Gothic cathedrals and to breathe from its lines " the last enchantments of the Middle Age."

In 1918 we, too, dreamed of unity. Wars were to cease. Nations, those artificial substitutes for real spiritual unions, were to abate their pretensions, and by surrendering a little of their sovereignty were to enter into a larger society and inherit a grander and less precarious life. It was a noble dream, worthy of our best selves. But, cheated by fears, plucked to earth by disappointment, and brought lower, I verily believe, than our true level, by listening to uninspired maxims, by timidly accepting commonplace people at their own exorbitant valuation, and by supposing that because they

are commonplace their voice must be the voice of
universal wisdom, we have deliberately chosen discord instead of unity. And so it has come to pass
that in no year since 1321, if Dante could have returned to life again, would he have found Christendom less unified than in 1921.

The tendency of Western civilization since the
Middle Ages has been towards disruption. I do not
say that this has not often been a healthful tendency. What is not fully realized, however, is that
the aspiration and the action of men, of leaders
fully as much as of masses, have been directed towards a different object from the object dear to the
mediæval mind. The object cherished by the mediæval mind was unity; the object most striven for
by men of the Renaissance and of the modern time
is diversity. Call it what you please — liberty, independence, self-expression, expansion, specializa-
tion, progress — the new ideal is exactly opposite
to the old. The Revival of Learning disturbed the
nice adjustment which the mediæval mind had
made between Christian tradition and Greek philosophy, the pagan element of the compound being
increased until the equipoise was broken. The Ref-
ormation would have been regarded by mediæval
Christians as a second fulfillment of the prophecy:
"They parted my garments among them, and upon
my vesture did they cast lots"; and they would

have lamented that the seamless unity of Christ's Church was destroyed. The shifting of authority from the few to the many, from monarchs and aristocrats to the sovereign people, all that age-long movement which we term the political revolution, a movement which began in the Middle Ages themselves and is still going on, — this too would have shocked the mediæval mind. The separation of the physical and historical sciences from philosophy, and the differentiation of the sciences from one another — processes that marked the seventeenth, eighteenth and nineteenth centuries and have been rich in material results — were contrary to mediæval ideas of unity in learning. A modern university would seem to a mediæval scholar something like a department store without a manager, or like a heterogeneous mass of machinery without motive power or any reference to production or locomotion. " What is it for? " he would ask, and " whither does it tend? " If he were to pick up the catalogue of some general publisher or a copy of the " Times Literary Supplement " (either the London or the New York "Times ") he would say: "This is chaos. There is no order among all these books. They have nothing in common, except commonness, and no particular tendency except a tendency to be particular."

Now, I am by no means inclined to glorify the

Middle Ages at the expense of modern civilization. When I read history I find myself almost always on the side of the Reformers, the Revolutionists, the Dissenters, the Apostles of Science. I have faith in Democracy. I am still holding on with both hands, in spite of many cruel disappointments and much pale apprehension, to the revolutionary doctrines of human equality and human perfectibility. I believe the world has made progress and will continue to make progress, and in saying this I am not thinking so much of mechanical improvement, or the combat against time and space, as of spiritual welfare. There is no reason to suppose that men were, in general, better or even happier in the Middle Ages than we were at the opening of the twentieth century.

Nevertheless, it is obvious that a bewildering and inexpressible contrast would appear to Dante if, across the gulf of these six hundred years, he were to revisit the glimpses of the moon. He would hardly recognize the world we live in as either Christian or civilized. In fact, it would not seem to him a world, or cosmos, at all, but a chaos of meaningless and restless change, with no unity of structure, direction, or purpose. He would entirely disapprove of those features of our life, precisely, in which most men now take the greatest pride. Our arrangements for physical comfort, our mechanical devices, would no doubt interest him, for he had an eye for such things in his own day; but he would, I fancy, regard them as having come between us and God. And when he looked into our political, educational, and religious systems, or fragments of systems and denials of system, he would turn away with condemnation written in the folds of his august brow.

We have made poor use of our eyes and ears and are stupid readers of history if we have not noticed that the rate of change has been much accelerated in recent years. Whether we applaud or regret the tendencies of our age, we must admit that they are increasingly centrifugal and that their velocity is increasing. It behooves us, therefore, to measure, if we can, the force and direction of these tendencies, or we may be swept by them whither we would not.

In order to make these measurements, we must find some point of departure, some place of relatively stable conditions. We should, if possible, go back to some position of unity, from which to estimate the extent of our diversity. There is no point of this kind nearer than the early part of the fourteenth century, and it is a singular advantage that no other period of the world's history has had its culture so accurately and yet broadly described in a single work. A strange thing, is it not, that a poem which professes to narrate a journey through Hell, Purgatory, and Heaven, should be actually a picture of human society in Italy? Strange that a poem whose theme is eternity should be our best means of understanding the fourteenth century! But stranger still is the case if we are right in thinking that no other poem or work of art whatsoever can help us so much to an understanding of our own country and our own times. In land-surveying, as in astronomy, the longer your base-line the more accurate will be your measurement of objects which, through distance or the intervention of impassable obstacles, are unattainable. So it is with measuring the force and direction of social movements. We can do it only by standing apart from them.

This great reason, among several others, is what gives so rich an educational value to the "Divine Comedy." Of these other reasons, I need mention only its intrinsic poetical worth and beauty and the fact that it, more fully than any other human creation, reveals the mind and heart of him who made it. As a gross and ready proof of its quality we may take its quotability. It is the most generally quoted of all poems, having great lines for all great occasions, and fine and subtle lines for many particular by-paths of thought and experience. In no respect, however, is it so remarkable as in its being, after all, not so much a work of art as a man speaking:

it is Dante himself. Not Homer, not Virgil, not
Shakespeare, not Milton, not Molière, so breathe in
their works as Dante breathes in his. The great reason, with which we are now concerned, however,
might be called its power as prophecy. The action
of prophecy is to "rebuke the world of sin, of
righteousness, and of judgment"; and this action
the "Divine Comedy" performs.

Thus it becomes evident that no other single work
of literature possesses so high an educational value
and should so certainly be included in any pro-
gramme of advanced education. Its inclusion would
be justified from yet another point of view. Modern attempts at education, especially in America,
often fail to produce satisfactory results because
they they are scattering and superficial. They do
not provide a center of effort with a large body of
material lying closely packed round that center,
and they do not require a discipline or a mastery
of technique sufficiently thorough to enable a student to fight his way through from the circumference to the center of this body of material. Energy
is squandered, and self-command is not attained.
The "Divine Comedy" offers itself as a center towards which a student may work his way by the
study of the Italian and Latin languages, the mythology of antiquity, the Bible, the Aristotelian
metaphysics and ethics, the "Summa" of Thomas

Aquinas, and the history of Christendom down to the year 1300, and then out again from center to circumference, through the æsthetic, scholastic, political, and religious revolutions of the Renaissance and the last three centuries, to a consideration of every large modern question that is not scientific. I do not say that a selection of the best Greek literature or of the best Latin literature might not serve the purpose as well. They have so served in the past, in the way they were taught in the English universities. I merely wish to suggest that the "Divine Comedy" has the advantage of being a single work, to equal the scope of which you would have to pile, for your Greek center, Plato upon Euripides and Euripides on Homer, and then add a dome of clouds and lightning for Aristophanes; and your Latin center would be at least equally composite. If a student will attach himself to Dante for three or four or five years, reading up to him and into him, and then away from him, trying to place himself in Dante's age and country, and then applying to modern conditions some of Dante's wisdom, he will be a well-educated man, except on that side alone which science affects.

It is the general complaint of the headmasters of private schools, the principals of public high schools, and the presidents of colleges, that education lacks a center. They have reluctantly given up the center which classical literature afforded and are afraid to adopt the one that natural science offers. They have here and there tried the ideal of public service, making the hub of the wheel consist of " civil government," or sociology, or economics, but the experiment fails because the hub is not big enough to accommodate all the spokes that a perfect wheel requires. And considering the immensity of scientific knowledge which has to be reckoned with, no one wheel is enough. Modern education must move forward on an axle sustained by two wheels, one constructed of scientific studies, the other of humanistic. I will back the teachers of science to construct their wheel on sound principles within the next thirty years; but unless the teachers of the humanities are willing to return to the old classical model they must look for a substitute. In case they think, as they apparently do, that the youth of today are too unmanageable or too feebleminded for the discipline of the ancient classics, they will find no substitute so well fitted for the purpose as the " Divine Comedy." In all American colleges and universities, as the statistics of elective choices show, the attempt is being made to find one center of humanistic training in English literature and another in a jumble of historico-politico-economic studies. The attempt fails in both directions, because in neither is there a sufficiently simple and yet difficult block of material at the heart of the subject. Dante furnishes such a block of education.

In religion, likewise, a fresh and sound impulse would be given to modern society by the study of Dante. The impact between the fluctuating modern mind and Dante's rigid theology would be tremendous. In Dante is made manifest not only the glory of historic orthodoxy, but its incompatibility with the deepest and sweetest human morality; the lifelessness of orthodoxy would be finally felt out by the touch of those sympathies which the heart of modern man cherishes as its real religion, and at last we should know where we stand with reference to the " rock of ages " on which Dante so firmly placed his feet. It is hardly to be supposed that the soft, flexible, and wary religious spirit of today, beautiful and variegated as a butterfly, ambitious as an eagle, tender as a dove, will settle permanently on that rock; rather will it learn what to avoid. At any rate, an acquaintance with something so stern and stationary would be instructive.

It is in the field of politics, however, that the study of Dante would be most fruitful in wisdom and entertainment. The amusement would be of that dry Aristophanic quality which tends to produce not laughter so much as grinding of teeth. There is joy in knowledge, but the first knowledge that comes to a disciple of Dante as he surveys the scene of contemporary politics is bitter. Our young people are complaining because all the great preachers and every living poet worthy of the name are telling them that this is an evil world, and that an abyss yawns ahead into which we shall all plunge, unless ———. The happiness natural to their youth is being poisoned. Well, I am afraid Dante would hold the cup still closer to their lips. And we must drink it out before it can be refilled, with the water of hope and strength. Dante's conception of the Kingdom of God as the goal of political and social life is unrelenting, for all its promise and splendor. No disciple of Dante can take a frivolous, easy-going view of social and political conditions. He can neither rest in selfish individualism nor trust in a dream of coöperative ease. The seriousness of Dante, his clear perception of the temporary character of all outward show and sensual satisfaction, lifts his disciples above vulgarity. They walk in the light of eternity, neither strutting nor creeping, for they have some perception of the soul's worth. In their lighter mood, they wonder what Dante, were he to come alive again, would write about America today. Whom of us, what living individuals and what historical personages, would he consign to Hell, and whom to Purgatory, and whom to Paradise? What ingenious and appropriate punishments would he invent for the grafter, the profiteer, the corrupt politician? What destiny of undying scorn would he devise for the voiceless neuter? What grim smile would he bestow, like a plague, upon the ostentatious upstart and the idle or much-divorced rich? In his "Paradise" there is the Rose of the Blessed, every petal the throne of a saint, and all as definitely fixed and assigned as are the desks in the United States Senate chamber, but otherwise occupied. He would not hesitate to evoke a corresponding pageant in a new "Inferno." Would he not repeat, with reference to our failure to enter the League of Nations, those bitter words which he applied to the Pope Celestine who preferred his own comfort to the welfare of the Church? —

> " Guardai, e vidi l'ombra di colui
>   Che fece per viltate il gran rifiuto."

I fancy his American epic would consist of two parts, which might be called the Cup of Purgation and the Cup of Healing. Whether proffered by a poet or by some consuming plague of war and disaster, we cannot put by the Cup of Purgation if we are ever to be found worthy to drink the Cup of Healing.

A LESSON FROM DANTE

There are two kinds of poets, between whom it is important that we should distinguish as completely and clearly as possible. On the one hand are the many who possess " the accomplishment of verse," often in rich profusion and not seldom with fine penetration into the realities of nature and life, yet of whom we cannot assert that they are great leaders of thought. We go to them for entertainment, relaxation, sensuous enjoyment, rather than for wisdom. On the other hand are the poets endowed with "the vision and the faculty divine," who are philosophers or teachers fully as much as they are givers of pleasure. It is not always the fortune of a philosopher to give pleasure nor the duty of an artist to make men wise; but the supreme poets have been those few in whom a perfect mastery of the powers of verse, its musical charm and its pictorial magic, was dominated by towering hearts and comprehensive intellects. Some of the Romantic poets of the nineteenth century, belonging to the class of entertainers rather than sages, made preposterous claims as teachers of wisdom. Even of poets who are much more indeed than purveyors of delight, even of Byron and Hugo, of Shelley and Musset, for example, is it not in vain that we expect a broadly based, profound, and tragically earnest interpretation of life? In every case something is lacking, either experience or learning or depth or seriousness. We dare not take these poets at their own valuation.

But there is another order of poets, few in number and scattered in time, whom we can hardly trust enough, whose authority we must acknowledge if we have any appreciation of what constitutes human grandeur. When they claim to have discovered truth we may rest assured that they not only mean what they say but have really found something which relates itself naturally to the body of thought that has grown up in their minds, something organic and vital. It is our misfortune and shame if we do not at least give them credit for being absolutely sincere. There is no plainer mark of shallowness or immaturity than to take them less than seriously. We may with confidence assume that what they wrote and permitted to stand in their names, when once they had attained complete stature as poets, is full of significance. In this order of poets Dante holds the most unquestioned place, and in his company are Milton, Goethe, Wordsworth.

When, therefore, Dante professes to be a Ghibelline, it behooves us to inquire very carefully what the implications of that name are. Of course, as a

Ghibelline, he believed that God had ordained two powers as rulers of the world, the Imperial power to govern men in secular affairs, and the Papal power to govern them in all that part of their spiritual life which could be regulated by an external authority. He believed that the efficiency of the Empire would be best maintained and developed if the Church kept hands off the machinery of politics, and that no Emperor should attempt to rule the Church. The fundamental idea of Dante's Ghibellinism, an idea that transcends the party strife of his time and even the mere relation between Church and State, is the idea of freedom: man's religious life should be free from secular interference; man's political life should be free from ecclesiastical control. But this conception of freedom, of immunities, sacred regions of personality, fields of activity guarded against this or that intrusion of power, involves the delimitation of a third protected area. It implies not only a separation between Church and State, but non-interference by either Church or State with a third power, namely the School.

The instruction which Dante had enjoyed, his knowledge of philosophy, mythology, history, and science, was obtained in large measure from sources that flowed long before the Christian era and the establishment of the Roman Empire. As

Milton says in " Comus," thinking perhaps of his own indebtedness to ancient Greece, the root of virtue itself

> " in another country "
> " Bore a bright golden flower, but not in this soil,"

so Dante dares to name Aristotle " the master of those who know," calling the roll of his " philosophic family," Socrates, Plato, Democritus, and many others, who " all admire and all honor him." Even in Dante's time, education was not wholly dependent on the Church, and the spirit of his Ghibellinism authorized him to turn for intellectual support to the schools of Greece, pre-Christian and extra-Roman though they were. We may be sure he would have resented and opposed with all the force of his indomitable character any attempt to prescribe what springs his mind should drink from.

But in an age when Dante dared to soar, other minds were forced to creep. His conception of freedom and of the necessity of distinguishing the three elements in which humanity ought to expatiate has been realized only with difficulty and after long delay. It spread mightily in the Renaissance, but is by no means universally adopted to-day, even though in most countries certain functions that used to be exercised by the Church are now definitely committed to the School. At first, and for a long time, it was of the Church, rather than of the State, that the School had to assert its independence. Slowly and imperfectly has the emancipation been accomplished. Many predictions were made that this separation would prove harmful to learning or to religion, and, though opinions differ, most candid observers would agree that these prophecies have not been fulfilled. No school or college or university which has once shaken off ecclesiastical control would willingly submit to it again. Church schools are notoriously inferior in the mental education they afford, and it is not at all obvious that they are superior in the moral result of their methods.

A danger peculiar to modern times, and more threatening than usual at present, is excessive control of the School by the State. For many persons the School has wholly or in part come to take the Church's place. It is the chief source of their idealism, their conscious morality, their intellectual life. We can no more afford to let the State make the School one of its branches than we could afford to let the State control the Church. " A free Church in a free State " is a conception for which Dante is in large measure to be thanked, and which he would understand and accept to-day. We are obliged to extend its significance so that it includes "a free School in a free State."

All are agreed, or so it is supposed, that politics

should be kept out of school. But are they? Have we not seen arrogant majorities assuming that their doctrines were the opinions of all good people and denouncing the doctrines of minorities as unpatriotic and un-American? Have we not seen legislatures, obsessed by panic alarm, trying to turn education into a drill in civic regularity? Patriotism is an excellent thing when it is enlightened and sincere, but an odious thing when it is fanatical or hypocritical. The virtuous quality in patriotism cannot be taught from a manual; the dangerous and false kind may be so taught. Teachers should not be obliged to pass a test in patriotism. The plan is absurd and would defeat its own end. If a candidate is conscientious, he may express scruples which in the judgment of a stupid examiner would debar him from the profession. If he is unprincipled, it makes no difference whether he is patriotic or not; he will pretend he is. Thus any test of this kind would operate against honest men to the advantage of the dishonest.

Because a teacher is paid by the State, it does not follow that the State should dictate in detail what subjects he shall teach or what his methods shall be. The very word School means a place of leisure, not, of course, leisure in the ordinary sense of the word, but rather freedom from interference. Certainly freedom is essential to the life of a school, — above all, freedom on the part of the teacher to exercise his personality, direct his influence, and feel out for knowledge as he sees fit. The more original, bold, and authoritative a teacher is, the better. He must not live with his eye upon any masters, whether they be the scholars' parents, or newspaper editors, or representatives of government.

When Dante needed a guide in the first part of his great pilgrimage of instruction, he received, for this elementary stage, not a chartered courier of the Church nor yet a delegate of the State, no angelic doctor and no exponent of the civil law, no saint and no emperor, but a teacher, who, though he "lived in Rome under the good Augustus," "vissi a Roma sotto'l buono Augusto" was more than Roman, and, though he dwelt not in the abode of the damned, was less than Christian. The poet, the man of letters, the scholar, the repository of culture, came to Dante neither from the Church nor from the State; he was free. And it was well for Dante and for the success of his journey that he could call Virgil "my master and my author, famous sage," "lo mio maestro e lo mio autore," "famoso saggio."

It should be the aim of every teacher to help his pupil on to freedom, freedom from fear of public opinion, from fear of the press, from fear of standing morally alone. All his efforts and hopes should bend forward to the hour when he can say to the youth, as Virgil said to Dante:

"Free, erect, and sound is thy judgment,
  And not to follow it would be unwise;
  Therefore be State and Church unto thyself."

"Libero, dritto, sano è lo tuo arbitrio,
  E fallo fôra non fare a suo senno;
  Per ch'io te sopra te corono e mitrio."

Dante was too great a poet, too awful in his
exactness, not to have meant by "corono e mitrio"
precisely what I have indicated in the translation.
Another poet might have used the words vaguely,
though the longer I study poetry the more I am convinced that great poets have always been in earnest,
seeing and hearing more precisely than other men
and employing language far more seriously. But
Dante, above all other poets, puts definitely sense
into every syllable he utters. And since he said both
"corono" and "mitrio," he meant to make a distinction. "I crown and mitre thee lord of thyself."
What is the distinction? It is very plain. The political ruler or Emperor is crowned; the spiritual ruler
or Pope is mitred. Virgil, deriving his authority
neither from Emperor nor from Pope, being independent of both, makes Dante a freeman of Empire and of Church. He has imparted to his pupil
knowledge of the world and also the wisdom that
fits him for communion with the saints. He has
grounded him in science, in history, in politics, and
winged him for his flight to higher spheres.